Digital Dawn

The Rise of New Business Realities

by

Harper Sinclair

Table of Contents

Navigating the Digital Frontier

The journey into the digital frontier is both exhilarating and daunting. For business leaders and entrepreneurs eager to forge ahead, this uncharted terrain offers unparalleled opportunities and challenges. The essence of this transformation is not merely technological but fundamentally strategic and operational at its core. It demands a reimagining of traditional business models, urging leaders to embrace a future where innovation and agility are paramount.

At the heart of this digital odyssey lies the recognition that the landscape of business is undergoing a seismic shift. The proliferation of digital technologies has unleashed a new era of competition and creativity. Companies that harness the power of this digital revolution position themselves at the vanguard of their industries, pioneering approaches that redefine what is possible.

The digital realm is replete with instances of disruptive innovation that have reshaped entire industries. This phenomenon is not confined to the tech giants of Silicon Valley but is a global narrative, with businesses across sectors leveraging digital tools to enhance efficiency, customer experience, and profitability. The implications of these changes are far-reaching, encouraging businesses to adapt or risk obsolescence.

Understanding the contours of the digital landscape is essential for navigating its complexities. The emergence of data analytics, artificial intelligence (AI), blockchain technology, and the Internet of Things (IoT) has set the stage for a new era of business operation and customer interaction. These technologies, while distinct, share the common thread of driving forward the capabilities of businesses in myriad and multifaceted ways.

The digital frontier is not solely about technology; it is equally about the culture of innovation and change it engenders. For businesses to thrive, they must cultivate an environment that fosters creativity, flexibility, and a willingness to experiment. This cultural shift is as crucial as any technological adoption, for it is the people within organizations who will navigate these changes and unlock new value.

Resistance to change is a natural human instinct, yet it represents a significant barrier to digital transformation. Leaders must therefore not only act as visionaries but also as champions of a digital mindset, guiding their teams through the uncertainties of change with clarity and confidence. It is through such leadership that businesses can transform challenges into stepping stones towards innovation and growth.

Developing a coherent digital strategy is not an option but a necessity in today's fast-paced environment. This strategy should be comprehensive, encompassing not just technological adoption but also the readiness of the workforce, the digitalization of customer experiences, and the organization's overall agility. It is this strategic foresight that empowers businesses to lead rather than follow in the digital domain.

Reinventing customer experiences in the digital age requires a deep understanding of the new ways in which people interact with technology and businesses. Personalization, fueled by data analytics, stands at the forefront of creating value for customers in ways that were previously unimaginable. This reconceptualization of engagement is a cornerstone of digital transformation efforts.

The digital landscape also introduces new challenges in marketing and branding. In a world inundated with information, standing out requires not only creativity but also strategic use of digital tools to reach and resonate with target audiences. The evolution of digital marketing underscores the necessity for businesses to adapt continually to the changing digital paradigms.

As workplaces transform, so too do the expectations and capabilities of the workforce. The digital age necessitates not just technological fluency but also a shift in the way work is conceptualized and executed. Creating a flexible, collaborative digital workplace is essential for fostering innovation and attracting the talent necessary to propel businesses forward.

Yet, the digital frontier is not without its ethical and legal quandaries. Privacy, security, and regulatory compliance pose significant challenges to businesses as they navigate the digital landscape. Understanding these complexities is paramount, as is the development of thoughtful strategies to address them. This understanding ensures that the digital transformation journey is not only innovative but also responsible and sustainable.

The path to digital transformation is illuminated by the successes of those who have navigated it skillfully. Case studies of digital innovation provide valuable insights and inspiration, demonstrating the transformative potential of strategic digital adoption. These narratives are not just stories of technology but of leadership, vision, and resilience.

Looking ahead, the digital frontier continues to expand with emerging technologies that promise to further transform the business landscape. Staying abreast of these developments and preparing for the next wave of digital disruption is crucial for leaders seeking to position their businesses for future success.

In conclusion, navigating the digital frontier requires a blend of strategic foresight, technological acumen, and leadership excellence. It is a journey defined by constant learning, adaptation, and a relentless pursuit of innovation. For those ready to embark on this journey, the reward is not just survival but the opportunity to redefine the boundaries of what is possible in the digital age.

The promise of the digital frontier is vast, teeming with opportunities for growth, innovation, and transformation. As we stand on the brink of this new era, the question is not whether to embark on this journey, but how to navigate it with vision, purpose, and agility. The future belongs to those who are ready to seize it, transforming the challenges of digital disruption into the building blocks of a reimagined, resilient, and thriving business landscape.

Chapter 1:
The Digital Revolution: An Overview

The onset of the Digital Revolution is redefining the boundaries of innovation, leadership, and strategic vision. It's not merely an era of technological advancements; it's a critical juncture where businesses must pivot to thrive or risk obsolescence. This chapter delves into the heart of the digital transformation, painting a broad strokes overview that encapsulates its essence and significance. Embracing digitalization isn't just about adopting new technologies; it's about cultivating a mindset that welcomes change, values data-driven decision-making, and understands the power of connectivity and automation in crafting compelling customer experiences. As we unpack the driving forces behind this transformative wave, from exponential increases in computing power to the ubiquitous access to information, you'll see how industries are being reshaped. But it's important to note, this is only the beginning. The true depth of digital disruption and its capacity to revolutionize how we do business, engage with customers, and lead our teams is explored in the chapters to come. Acknowledging the digital revolution's vastness and its profound impact on the commercial landscape is the first step in harnessing its potential. In doing so, you, as a forward-thinking leader, are better positioned to navigate this new frontier, leveraging digital transformation as a formidable tool in crafting your organization's future.

The Driving Forces Behind Digital Transformation

In today's rapidly evolving business landscape, understanding the driving forces behind digital transformation is crucial for forward-thinking leaders. The revolution sweeping across industries is not just about technology; it's about how these technologies are harnessed to reshape businesses, reinvent customer experiences, and redefine the competitive edge.

At the heart of this transformation is the exponential growth of data. Every click, swipe, and interaction generates insights that, when properly analyzed and leveraged, can propel businesses to new heights. This data-driven approach allows businesses to understand their customers more deeply, predict trends, and make informed decisions that were previously beyond reach.

Another significant driver is the advancement in cloud computing. The scalability and flexibility offered by cloud technologies enable organizations of all sizes to access powerful computing resources without significant upfront investments. This democratization of technology spurs innovation, fosters agility, and allows companies to adapt quickly to changing market demands.

Consumer expectations are also reshaping the business landscape. Today's customers demand more personalized, convenient, and seamless experiences. They expect to interact with brands across multiple channels while receiving consistent service. This push towards customer-centricity compels businesses to rethink their strategies, operations, and how they engage with customers.

Competition, while always a factor in business, has taken on new dimensions in the digital age. The threat no longer comes just from traditional competitors but also from digital start-ups that can disrupt entire industries with innovative business models and technologies.

This has led established companies to embrace digital transformation not just as a means of survival but as a way to innovate and lead.

The rapid pace of technological advancements is a double-edged sword. On one hand, it offers unprecedented opportunities for growth and innovation. On the other, it presents a challenge for businesses to keep up and integrate new technologies effectively. Artificial intelligence (AI), machine learning, blockchain, and the Internet of Things (IoT) are just a few examples of technologies that are shaping the future of business in ways we are just beginning to understand.

Regulatory and compliance requirements also play a critical role in driving digital transformation. As governments and regulatory bodies worldwide respond to the challenges and opportunities posed by digital technologies, businesses must navigate a complex landscape of regulations to ensure compliance while leveraging digital strategies for growth.

The environmental and societal pressures are urging businesses to adopt more sustainable and responsible practices. Digital technologies offer innovative ways to reduce waste, improve energy efficiency, and create more sustainable business models. This shift is not just about corporate responsibility but also about meeting the changing expectations of consumers, employees, and stakeholders.

The workforce itself is a driving force behind digital transformation. As digital natives become a larger part of the workforce, their expectations for a technologically sophisticated and flexible working environment encourage businesses to digitalize operations, communication, and collaboration practices. This shift towards a more digital workplace fosters innovation and attracts top talent.

Globalization has intensified competition but also opened new markets and opportunities for businesses willing to adapt and transform digitally. The ability to operate, compete, and collaborate on a global scale is facilitated by digital technologies, making digital transformation a strategic imperative for businesses looking to expand their reach.

Innovation in payment technologies and financial services, such as fintech and blockchain, has transformed how transactions are conducted, secured, and recorded. These innovations not only enhance efficiency but also open new avenues for product and service offerings, further driving businesses towards digital transformation.

The convergence of physical and digital worlds, through technologies such as augmented reality (AR) and virtual reality (VR), provides businesses with new ways to engage customers and create immersive experiences. This blurring of lines between what's physical and digital pushes companies to innovate and transform to stay relevant in a rapidly changing world.

Lastly, the drive for digital transformation is also propelled by the desire to gain a competitive advantage through innovation. The ability to rapidly prototype, test, and iterate on new ideas and products using digital tools enables businesses to stay ahead of the curve and differentiate themselves in crowded markets.

In conclusion, the forces driving digital transformation are multifaceted, encompassing technological advancements, shifting consumer expectations, regulatory pressures, and the evolving global business landscape. For leaders and entrepreneurs, staying abreast of these drivers and understanding how they impact your business is essential for navigating the challenges and seizing the opportunities of the digital age. By embracing digital transformation, you can redefine your business, drive growth, and lead in the new digital economy.

As we move forward, it's clear that digital transformation is no longer an option but a necessity. The question for today's leaders is not if they should embark on this journey but how they can do so most effectively. Embracing change, leveraging new technologies, and fostering a culture of innovation are key to thriving in this new digital era. Let's embark on this journey with confidence, knowing that the future belongs to those who are prepared to reinvent themselves and their businesses for the digital age.

How Digital Disruption Is Reshaping Industries

In the heart of our digital epoch lies a profound transformation, marked by the rapid evolution of technology and its far-reaching impact across every sector. This section delves into the myriad ways in which digital disruption is not just altering, but fundamentally reshaping industries. It's a clarion call for business leaders and entrepreneurs to adapt, innovate, and thrive amidst the whirlwind of change.

Digital disruption, at its core, is the change that occurs when new digital technologies and business models affect the value proposition of existing goods and services. It's a phenomenon that has led to the emergence of new leaders in several sectors while pushing traditional entities to the brink of irrelevance. The power of such disruption stems from its ability to democratize information, streamline processes, and customize experiences at a scale previously unimaginable.

Consider the impact of e-commerce on retail. Brick-and-mortar stores, once the bastions of shopping, now compete with digital giants capable of offering a wider selection, better prices, and the convenience of shopping from anywhere, anytime. This shift has not only changed consumer behavior but also forced retailers to reimagine their strategies, integrating online and offline experiences to create omnichannel solutions.

Similarly, the media and entertainment industries have been revolutionized by streaming services, which leverage data analytics to offer personalized content recommendations. This has challenged traditional television and film business models, emphasizing the need for adaptability in content creation, distribution, and monetization strategies.

The finance sector is another domain experiencing the seismic shifts of digital disruption. Fintech startups, utilizing blockchain, artificial intelligence, and advanced data analytics, are redefining banking, payments, and investment services. This has pressed established financial institutions to accelerate their digital transformation efforts, adopting more customer-centric approaches and innovative technologies to stay competitive.

In healthcare, digital technology is empowering patients and providers alike with tools for better management of health and disease. From telemedicine and wearable devices to AI-driven diagnostics, the digital revolution is making healthcare more accessible, personalized, and efficient. This shift not only improves patient outcomes but also opens new avenues for service delivery and engagement.

Manufacturing, too, has entered a new era with the advent of Industry 4.0, characterized by smart factories where interconnected devices and systems autonomously communicate and learn from each other. This digital transformation is optimizing production processes, reducing waste, and facilitating unprecedented levels of customization.

The thread that weaves through each of these industry transformations is the incredible pace of change, spurred by the relentless advancement of technology. For businesses, this means that the ability to quickly adapt and innovate is no longer optional but a necessity for survival and success. The stakes are high, and the time to act is now.

Yet, amidst these challenges lies a trove of opportunity. Digital disruption is not just about survival; it's about seizing the chance to redefine industries, creating new value for customers, and carving out leadership positions in emerging spaces. The businesses that succeed in this endeavor are the ones that view technology not as a threat but as an enabler of innovation and growth.

To navigate this landscape, business leaders must foster a culture of continuous learning, encourage experimentation, and remain vigilantly attuned to technological developments and customer expectations. Equally important is the ability to forge strategic partnerships that can expand capabilities and accelerate the path to innovation.

Embracing digital disruption also means rethinking how value is delivered to customers. In a world where customer experiences often dictate success or failure, businesses must leverage data analytics, AI, and other digital tools to provide personalized, engaging, and seamless experiences across all touchpoints.

Moreover, sustainability and social responsibility have become integral to business success. Digital technology offers powerful ways to achieve these goals, from optimizing resource use to enhancing transparency and accountability. Businesses that integrate these values into their digital transformation efforts will not only thrive but also contribute to a healthier planet and society.

In conclusion, the reshaping of industries by digital disruption is a phenomenon that contains as much promise as it does challenge. For forward-thinking business leaders and entrepreneurs, it represents a unique opportunity to lead change, rather than merely react to it. By embracing digital transformation, businesses can not only survive but thrive, shaping a future that is innovative, sustainable, and responsive to the needs of a rapidly changing world.

The journey of digital transformation is complex, fraught with challenges but also ripe with opportunities. As industries continue to evolve, adaptability, innovation, and visionary leadership will be the hallmarks of those who not only withstand the forces of disruption but also harness them to forge new paths forward. Let's embark on this journey together, with the resolve to transform challenges into opportunities and reshape the future of our industries.

As we delve deeper into the specifics of digital transformation in subsequent chapters, keep in mind that the key to leveraging digital disruption lies not in technology alone but in how it's applied to create real value for businesses and their customers. The future belongs to those who can envision and execute a digital strategy that aligns with their core strengths and the emerging needs of the market. The potential is limitless, and the time to act is now.

Chapter 2:
Understanding Digital Transformation

In the grand narrative of modern business, understanding digital transformation is akin to discovering a new compass that redefines the journey toward uncharted territories of growth and innovation. It's not just about adopting new technologies; it's a profound realignment of business models, strategies, and operations around the digital world's potentials and challenges. At its core, digital transformation involves a radical rethinking of how an organization uses technology, people, and processes to fundamentally change business performance. It's this transformative journey from traditional to digital that not only enhances efficiency but also unlocks new avenues of value creation and competitive advantage. With an ever-expanding digital landscape, the role of data and analytics becomes increasingly pivotal, offering unprecedented insights into customer behaviors and operational effectiveness. Similarly, the shift from traditional business models to ones that are digitally forward-thinking is not merely optional but essential for survival and success in today's fast-paced market environments. This chapter will guide you through the essential concepts of digital transformation, shedding light on its significance, the mechanisms driving it, and how it's shaping the very fabric of industries across the globe. Understanding this transformation is the first step toward mastering it, setting the stage for a journey of innovation, resilience, and unparalleled growth in the digital age.

The Role of Data and Analytics

In the journey towards digital transformation, data and analytics emerge as pivotal beacons, guiding the path for businesses adapting to the digital era. As we delve into this critical aspect of digital transformation, it's essential to recognize that data isn't just numbers or facts; it's the lifeblood that powers innovative strategies, drives decision-making, and creates competitive advantages in today's digitally dominated marketplace. The role of data and analytics in business today cannot be overstated; it's akin to navigating a vast ocean with precision and foresight.

Data analytics transforms raw data into actionable insights, allowing businesses to understand customer behavior, predict trends, optimize operations, and make informed decisions swiftly. This process is integral to sculpting a digital strategy that's robust, flexible, and aligned with the dynamic needs of the market. Imagine having the foresight to anticipate market trends before they occur or the ability to tailor customer experiences in real-time based on their interactions. This level of insight is what positions businesses at the forefront of innovation.

However, harnessing the power of data and analytics is not without its challenges. It demands a shift from traditional decision-making processes, often based on intuition or past experiences, to a data-driven approach that leans heavily on insights derived from data analytics. This transition requires not only the right tools and technologies but also a cultural shift within the organization towards valuing data as a critical asset.

The integration of data analytics into business operations enables organizations to become more agile, responsive, and efficient. For instance, in supply chain management, analytics can provide real-time insights into inventory levels, demand forecasting, and supplier performance, leading to improved operational efficiencies and cost reductions. Similarly, in customer service, data analytics can help identify patterns in customer inquiries or issues, enabling more proactive and personalized service solutions.

Moreover, the strategic application of data and analytics can fuel innovation by identifying new market opportunities, emerging trends, and areas for product or service enhancements. Businesses that are proactive in analyzing and acting on their data can not only stay ahead of the curve but also disrupt their industries by setting new standards and expectations.

Yet, the effective use of data and analytics extends beyond operational efficiency and innovation. It plays a crucial role in risk management by enabling businesses to identify potential threats and vulnerabilities within their operations, market trends, or the broader economic landscape. With the right analytics tools, organizations can simulate various scenarios and assess the potential impact of different strategies, making risk management more predictive and strategic.

Privacy and data protection are also paramount in the age of data and analytics. With increasing volumes of data being collected and analyzed, businesses must navigate the complex landscape of global data protection regulations and ensure the ethical use of data. This not only involves compliance with legal standards but also building trust with customers and stakeholders by demonstrating a commitment to protecting their data.

Furthermore, the democratization of data within an organization is an essential step towards fully leveraging the potential of data analytics. This means making data accessible to employees across departments, empowering them with the right tools and training to use this data effectively. By fostering a culture that encourages data-driven decision-making at all levels, businesses can unlock innovative ideas and solutions from within their own ranks.

The journey towards becoming a data-driven organization is continuous and evolving. It entails investing in the right technologies, such as cloud computing, AI, and machine learning, which can enhance the capability to collect, process, and analyze data at an unprecedented scale and speed. Additionally, it requires a steadfast commitment to building and nurturing a team skilled in data analysis and interpretation.

Leadership plays a critical role in this transformation. Leaders must champion the importance of data and analytics, setting a vision that integrates data into the DNA of the organization. They must also navigate the challenges of change management, ensuring that their teams are aligned, equipped, and motivated to embrace a data-centric approach.

In conclusion, the role of data and analytics in digital transformation is undeniably central. As businesses continue to navigate the complexities of the digital landscape, their ability to leverage data intelligently and innovatively will determine their success and sustainability. The path forward requires a holistic approach that encompasses technology, culture, leadership, and a steadfast commitment to leveraging data for strategic decision-making and innovation. By embracing data and analytics, businesses are not just adapting to the digital age; they are shaping it.

Embracing data and analytics is not merely a strategic choice but a necessity in the digital age. The insights derived from data can illuminate pathways to innovation, efficiencies, and competitive advantages that were previously obscured. As we forge ahead in this digital era, the organizations that can effectively harness the power of data and analytics will lead the charge, shaping the future of industries and redefining what it means to be successful in the digital world.

The multifaceted role of data and analytics in shaping digital transformation strategies underscores its importance. From improving customer experiences and operational efficiencies to fostering innovation and managing risks, data and analytics are indispensable tools in a leader's arsenal. As forward-thinking leaders and entrepreneurs, embracing the power of data and analytics is pivotal in navigating the digital transformation journey successfully.

The Shift from Traditional to Digital Business Models

The digital age is upon us, reshaping every facet of our lives, including the way businesses operate and create value. At the heart of this transformation is the shift from traditional business models, which have shaped our economic landscape for decades, to dynamic, digital models that are redefining the rules of engagement in the market. This shift is not merely optional; it's essential for sustainability and growth in an increasingly digital world.

Understanding this transition requires us to acknowledge the limitations of traditional business models. Historically, these models have relied heavily on physical assets, linear growth strategies, and a one-size-fits-all approach to customer service. However, as technological advancements accelerate, these traditional frameworks can no longer keep pace with the rapid changes in consumer behavior, global market pressures, and the speed of innovation.

The essence of digital business models lies in their ability to leverage digital technologies to enhance efficiency, create value in new ways, and deliver personalized experiences at scale. This means rethinking how resources are utilized, how value is created, and how relationships with customers are built and maintained. In doing so, businesses unlock opportunities for growth that were previously unimaginable.

At the core of digital transformation is data. The ability to collect, analyze, and act on data in real-time allows businesses to make informed decisions, predict market trends, and tailor experiences to meet individual customer needs. This data-centric approach is a stark departure from the intuition-based strategies that dominated the traditional business landscape.

Moreover, digital business models thrive on agility and flexibility. Unlike their traditional counterparts, which often struggle to adapt to change due to their size and structure, digital models are designed to pivot quickly in response to market demands. This agility is critical in an environment where consumer preferences and technological capabilities evolve at lightning speed.

Personalization is another hallmark of digital business models. In a world inundated with generic advertising and impersonal service, the ability to offer personalized experiences stands out as a significant competitive advantage. Digital technologies enable businesses to understand and anticipate individual customer needs, creating a level of engagement and loyalty that was once out of reach.

The shift to digital also necessitates a reevaluation of value creation. Traditional models often focus on extracting value in linear ways—manufacturing products, providing services, and selling directly to consumers. Digital models, in contrast, explore innovative revenue streams, including subscription services, platform-based economies, and freemium models, among others. These approaches not only diversify income but also strengthen customer relationships by offering continuous value.

Adopting a digital business model also opens the door to global markets. Digital platforms and e-commerce solutions eliminate geographical barriers, allowing even the smallest businesses to reach international audiences. This global perspective is vital for growth but also introduces new challenges in understanding and catering to diverse market needs.

The transition is not without its obstacles. Legacy systems, organizational culture, and resistance to change can hinder the shift to a digital model. Leaders must champion the cause, demonstrating a commitment to digital transformation through strategic investment, workforce training, and a willingness to experiment and learn from failures.

Collaboration plays a crucial role in the digital landscape. Traditional models often operate in silos, with limited interaction across departments or with external partners. Digital models, however, flourish through collaboration, leveraging partnerships and ecosystems to expand capabilities and reach. This interconnected approach amplifies innovation and accelerates growth.

Importantly, the shift to digital is an ongoing journey, not a destination. Technology continues to evolve, and with it, so too must business models. Staying ahead means being attuned to technological advancements, consumer trends, and global shifts, ready to adapt and innovate in response.

As we delve deeper into the digital age, the divide between traditional and digital business models will grow increasingly pronounced. Those who choose to embrace digital transformation will find themselves better positioned to compete in this new era, marked by unprecedented opportunities for innovation, growth, and connection.

The journey toward digital transformation can be daunting, but it's also exhilarating. The shift from traditional to digital business models is not just about survival; it's about thriving in a world of endless possibilities. It's an invitation to reimagine what your business can be and to take bold steps toward that vision. The future belongs to those who are ready to seize the opportunities of the digital age.

In navigating this shift, remember that you're not alone. Across industries, leaders are wrestling with similar challenges and chasing similar opportunities. The insights and strategies shared here aim to equip you with the knowledge to lead your organization with confidence through this transformation. Prepare to innovate, disrupt, and redefine the very essence of your business.

The digital frontier awaits. Are you ready to lead your business into the future? The time to act is now, leveraging the power of digital technologies to reshape your business model and embark on a journey of continuous transformation. The rewards extend beyond financial gains to lasting impact and leadership in a digitally driven world.

Chapter 3:
The Technologies Shaping Our Future

In this illuminative chapter, we dive deep into the vast ocean of emerging technologies that hold the promise of reshaping our future, offering a beacon of light for businesses poised on the edge of tomorrow. As we navigate through the intricacies of digital transformation, it's pivotal to understand that the tools and technologies at our disposal are not just facilitators of change, but architects of a new era. At the heart of this transformation, **Artificial Intelligence (AI)**, **Blockchain**, and the **Internet of Things (IoT)** stand as pillars upon which the future of business innovation rests. These are not mere buzzwords, but potent forces driving us towards uncharted territories of operational efficiency, transparency, and connectivity. By delving into each technology's potential, we explore how AI's predictive capacities and blockchain's unassailable integrity are setting the stage for a more interconnected and intelligent world. Meanwhile, IoT's ability to infuse everyday objects with digital life is redefining the boundaries between the physical and digital realms. As we anticipate these shifts, it's crucial for leaders to harness these technologies, not as a means to an end, but as vital companions in the journey towards a resilient and thriving digital ecosystem. This chapter aims to equip you with an understanding of these technologies not just as tools, but as transformative forces that demand a reimagining of business strategies in the face of relentless change.

Artificial Intelligence (AI) and Its Impact on Business

In today's rapidly advancing digital landscape, Artificial Intelligence (AI) stands at the forefront of technologies that are reshaping the way businesses operate, innovate, and interact with their customers. As an integral component of the digital transformation era, AI is not just a tool for automating processes but a transformative force that allows businesses to unlock unprecedented opportunities for growth, efficiency, and competitive advantage. This technology's ability to analyze vast amounts of data, identify patterns, and make informed decisions is revolutionizing industries by enhancing personalized customer experiences, optimizing operations, and creating new business models. For visionary business leaders and entrepreneurs, embracing AI means not only staying relevant in their respective markets but also leading the charge towards a future where technology and human ingenuity combine to solve complex problems and create value in new and exciting ways. The impact of AI on business is profound, urging companies to adapt and innovate. In doing so, they will discover the immense potential of AI to drive success, foster innovation, and ultimately, shape a future that leverages the full spectrum of digital capabilities at our disposal.

The Basics of AI and Machine Learning In this digital epoch, the reverberations of Artificial Intelligence (AI) and Machine Learning (ML) are omnipresent, reshaping industries and redefining the paradigms of business operations. Delving into the essentials of AI and ML is not just an academic pursuit but a strategic imperative for leaders aiming to navigate their enterprises through the tempestuous seas of digital transformation. At its core, AI is about creating machines that can perform tasks that typically require human intelligence. This includes problem-solving, recognizing patterns, understanding natural language, and learning from experience.

Machine Learning, a subset of AI, takes this a step further by enabling computers to learn and adapt through experience without being explicitly programmed for every task. The essence of ML lies in its ability to translate vast amounts of data into actionable insights, automating decision-making processes and unlocking new realms of efficiency and innovation.

Understanding the basics of these technologies is foundational. AI and ML algorithms power everything from search engines and recommendation systems to autonomous vehicles and sophisticated diagnostics tools in healthcare. They're at the heart of predictive analytics, enabling businesses to forecast trends and customer behaviors with unprecedented precision.

The proliferation of data is the fuel that propels AI and ML. With the advent of digital technologies, the volume of data generated by businesses and consumers has skyrocketed. This data, when harnessed properly, serves as the bedrock upon which effective AI and ML systems are built. Consequently, mastering data analytics is not optional but essential for leaders and entrepreneurs in the digital age.

Implementing AI and ML within an organization demands a strategic approach. It requires not only technical acumen but also a deep understanding of business processes and objectives. Successful integration of AI and ML technologies hinges on aligning them with your business strategy, ensuring they contribute directly to achieving your company's goals.

Leadership plays a critical role in this integration process. Embracing AI and ML necessitates fostering a culture of innovation within the organization. Leaders must champion these technologies, encouraging experimentation and learning. Equally important is managing the change, addressing concerns, and preparing the workforce for the transformations these technologies entail.

The ethical implications of AI and ML are profound and multifaceted. As these technologies assume greater decision-making roles, questions of bias, privacy, and accountability become increasingly critical. Business leaders must navigate these ethical minefields with a clear, principled approach, ensuring that AI and ML applications respect human rights and societal norms.

On a practical level, starting with AI and ML involves identifying use cases that offer significant value and are feasible. This often means focusing on areas where data is abundant and the potential for automation or enhanced decision-making is high. Experimentation and pilot projects can reveal what works, facilitating a scalable, impactful deployment.

Training and talent development are pivotal. The scarcity of AI and ML expertise is a significant hurdle. Investing in education and fostering a culture of continuous learning are vital strategies for building the needed capabilities within your organization. Partnering with academic institutions, technology providers, and specialized consultancies can also bridge the talent gap.

Metrics and measurement are essential for gauging the success of AI and ML initiatives. Clear benchmarks and performance indicators must be established from the outset, allowing leaders to track progress, iterate on strategies, and demonstrate the value of these investments to stakeholders.

Concerning data strategy, its importance cannot be overstated. Effective AI and ML applications are predicated on high-quality, well-managed data. This necessitates robust data governance practices, ensuring data integrity, security, and compliance with ever-evolving regulatory landscapes.

Look beyond the immediate. The journey of integrating AI and ML into your business is not merely about solving current challenges but also about anticipating the future. It's about building a foundation that allows your business to adapt and thrive in an increasingly unpredictable digital landscape. This forward-looking approach is what distinguishes leaders from followers in the digital age.

Innovation through AI and ML is a journey, not a destination. As these technologies evolve, so too must the ways in which businesses apply them. Continual learning, adaptation, and strategic foresight are key. By embracing AI and ML, businesses can not only enhance their current operations but also unlock new pathways to innovation and growth.

The dialogue about AI and ML is burgeoning with opportunities and challenges. For the forward-thinking business leader, understanding these technologies is more than a technical imperative—it's a strategic advantage. It represents a commitment to leading through the digital revolution, leveraging the power of AI and ML to forge a future that is prosperous, sustainable, and equitable.

The integration of AI and ML into business strategies marks a significant leap towards digital transformation. For leaders willing to embrace these technologies, the rewards are manifold. With AI and ML, businesses can achieve levels of efficiency, innovation, and customer satisfaction that were previously unimaginable. It's an exciting time to be at the helm of a digital-driven enterprise, steering it towards a future where technology and human ingenuity converge to create unparalleled value and opportunities.

AI in Practice: Real-World Business Applications As you've traversed the burgeoning landscape of digital transformation, the omnipresence of artificial intelligence (AI) in reshaping business operations cannot be overstated. Its implications are profound, making it an indispensable asset for leaders looking to fortify their enterprises against the challenges of tomorrow. The real-world applications of AI are as diverse as they are transformative, marking a paradigm shift in how businesses interact with their customers, optimize operations, and innovate for the future.

Consider the realm of customer service, where AI has revolutionized the traditional support model. Through the use of chatbots and virtual assistants, businesses can offer personalized, 24/7 support to customers around the globe. This not only enhances customer satisfaction but also significantly reduces operational costs. The ability of these AI-driven tools to learn from interactions and improve over time ensures that the quality of service continually evolves, setting a new benchmark in customer engagement.

AI's impact extends into the heart of decision-making processes as well. Predictive analytics, powered by AI, enables businesses to anticipate customer needs, market shifts, and potential operational bottlenecks with unprecedented accuracy. This foresight allows for proactive strategies, ensuring businesses remain competitive and agile in a dynamic market environment. The power to predict and act on future trends is no longer a luxury but a necessity in the digital age.

Marketing strategies have been equally transformed by AI's capabilities. Personalization, at a scale previously unimaginable, is now possible thanks to advances in machine learning and data analytics. Businesses can tailor their messaging, promotions, and recommendations to individual consumers, dramatically increasing engagement and conversion rates. This level of individualized marketing was once the domain of anecdotal narratives but is now a quantifiable and actionable strategy, thanks to AI.

Moreover, AI has made significant strides in operational efficiency. Through the automation of repetitive and time-consuming tasks, AI allows employees to focus on higher-value activities that require human insight and creativity. This shift not only boosts productivity but also enhances job satisfaction by removing mundane tasks from the workday. Industries ranging from manufacturing to finance have begun to realize the benefits of this application, reinventing their operational models around AI's capabilities.

The advent of AI in risk management presents another frontier where its implications are far-reaching. By analyzing vast datasets and identifying patterns that may elude human analysis, AI tools can help in predicting and mitigating potential risks. This capability is invaluable in sectors like finance and healthcare, where predictive insights can lead to better investment decisions or improved patient outcomes, respectively.

In the creative industries, AI has emerged as a collaborator, expanding the boundaries of what's possible. From generating original music and artwork to drafting creative content, AI tools are inspiring new forms of creativity and transforming the creative process. This synergy between human and machine creativity will undoubtedly shape the future of creative work, blurring the lines between technology and art.

The role of AI in developing sustainable solutions cannot be ignored. As businesses face increasing pressure to operate sustainably, AI offers powerful tools for optimizing energy use, reducing waste, and enhancing supply chain efficiencies. By leveraging AI's ability to analyze and optimize complex systems, companies can achieve their sustainability goals and reduce their ecological footprint.

Supply chain management has also benefitted from AI's intervention. With predictive analytics, businesses can anticipate supply chain disruptions and optimize inventory levels, ensuring product availability and customer satisfaction. The integration of AI in supply chain logistics is streamlining operations, reducing costs, and enhancing transparency across the board.

The impact of AI on healthcare is transformative, offering hope and innovation in equal measure. From diagnostics to personalized treatment plans, AI is revolutionizing patient care. Its ability to analyze medical data and uncover insights can lead to early detection of diseases, more effective treatments, and personalized healthcare journeys that were once deemed impossible.

Looking toward the sector of education, AI is democratizing learning by personalizing education at scale. Intelligent tutoring systems can adapt to the individual learning pace and style of each student, ensuring that educational content is accessible and engaging for all. This personalization of learning is a critical step towards briditing educational disparities and fostering a lifelong love for learning among students.

In the realm of security, AI's role is rapidly expanding. From cybersecurity solutions that protect against sophisticated digital threats to physical security systems that can predict and prevent incidents, AI is a cornerstone of modern security strategies. The ability to analyze patterns and predict threats in real-time is a game-changer, offering unprecedented levels of protection in a world where security concerns are ever-evolving.

AI's contribution to research and development (R&D) is sparking innovation across industries. By accelerating the pace of research, AI tools help in identifying new materials, drugs, and technologies faster than ever before. This speed in discovery and development is crucial in sectors like pharmaceuticals, where accelerated pathways to new treatments can save lives.

In the world of entertainment, AI is shaping content creation and consumption in unprecedented ways. From personalized recommendations to AI-generated content, the entertainment industry is leveraging AI to create more engaging and immersive experiences for audiences. This evolution is redefining entertainment, making it more interactive and tailored to individual preferences.

As we stand at the cusp of this AI-driven era, the opportunity for innovation and transformation across all spheres of business is immense. AI's role in driving efficiency, enhancing customer experience, and fostering innovation is undeniable. For forward-thinking leaders and entrepreneurs, the adoption and integration of AI into their business strategies is not just an option but a strategic imperative for sustained success in the digital age. Embracing AI is our collective leap toward a future where businesses not only survive the challenges of digital transformation but thrive amidst them, setting new benchmarks of excellence and innovation.

Blockchain: Beyond Cryptocurrency

In the transformative landscape of digital technology, blockchain emerges as a beacon of potential far beyond its original application in cryptocurrency. As business leaders, the exploration of blockchain's capabilities can unlock unparalleled efficiency and trust in transactions, mark an evolution in data management, and foster innovation across various sectors. This technology, at its core, provides a decentralized ledger, fundamentally altering our approach to data integrity and sharing. The implications for businesses are profound, offering a new realm of transparency in operations, supply chain management, and beyond. Imagine a world where contracts are executed automatically, supply chains are seamlessly transparent, and digital identities are secure and immutable. Blockchain stands as a pivotal technology in the digital transformation journey, challenging leaders to reimagine operational processes and business models. The strategic integration of blockchain technology can serve as a cornerstone in building resilient, transparent, and efficient systems that not only drive competitive advantage but also uphold the highest standards of trust and integrity in the digital age.

Understanding Blockchain Technology As we dive deeper into the digital age, business leaders and entrepreneurs are constantly seeking disruptive technologies that can provide a competitive edge and foster innovation within their industries. Blockchain technology stands out as a revolutionary force, capable of reshaping the global business landscape far beyond its initial application in cryptocurrency. Understanding its mechanics, potential, and implications is crucial for any forward-thinking business practitioner.

The essence of blockchain is its ability to provide a decentralized, secure, and immutable ledger of transactions. This capability offers unprecedented transparency and trust in a digital transaction, which traditional centralized systems struggle to provide. At its core, blockchain is a distributed database or ledger that is open to anyone. Every participant in the network has access to the entire database and its complete history. No single participant controls the data or the information. Once a transaction is entered in the ledger, it is secured using cryptographic technologies, ensuring that it cannot be altered, making blockchain technology a veritable truth machine in the digital era.

One of the most compelling attributes of blockchain technology is its potential to drastically reduce or eliminate fraud and errors, streamline administrative processes, and reduce costs. These features are particularly relevant in industries where secure and immutable record-keeping is critical, such as financial services, healthcare, and supply chain management. By enabling direct interactions between parties in a digital environment, blockchain eliminates the need for intermediaries, leading to faster and more cost-effective transactions.

Moreover, blockchain technology fosters transparency and enhances security. Its decentralized nature ensures that no single entity can control the entire network, making it resistant to censorship and less vulnerable to hacking or corruption. Every transaction on a blockchain is visible to all participants and cannot be changed once recorded. This level of transparency builds trust among users and can significantly enhance the accountability and integrity of digital transactions.

Yet, understanding blockchain is not without its challenges. The technology's concepts and terminology—such as smart contracts, consensus mechanisms, and cryptographic hash functions—can be daunting for non-specialists. However, grasping these basic concepts is essential for harnessing blockchain's potential and considering its application in various business contexts. A smart contract, for instance, is a self-executing contract with the terms of the agreement directly written into lines of code. This feature can automate complex processes and agreements, providing efficiency and security that traditional contracts often lack.

The decentralized nature of blockchain calls for a new approach to governance and collaboration. Implementing blockchain technology within an organization or across a sector involves navigating cultural and organizational shifts. It requires a consensus not only on the technical aspects but also on the governance models that underpin the technology's deployment. Engaging with blockchain demands an understanding that extends beyond technology to encompass strategic, operational, and ethical considerations.

Business leaders pondering over blockchain's relevance must also consider the scalability issues. As blockchain networks grow and the number of transactions increases, there are concerns about the technology's ability to scale effectively. However, ongoing technological advancements and the development of new consensus mechanisms are addressing these challenges, promising more scalable solutions that could support global business operations.

Another critical aspect for business practitioners is the regulatory environment surrounding blockchain. Regulatory frameworks for blockchain technology are still in development, and legal uncertainties can pose significant challenges. Navigating this evolving landscape requires a proactive approach, engaging with regulatory bodies and staying abreast of new developments to anticipate and adapt to changes in legal requirements.

The environmental impact of blockchain, particularly the energy-intensive process of mining digital currencies like Bitcoin, has raised concerns. It's crucial for leaders to consider sustainable practices and explore energy-efficient alternatives in blockchain technologies, aligning with broader corporate social responsibility and sustainability goals.

However, despite these challenges, the potential applications of blockchain extend far beyond cryptocurrency. From enhancing supply chain transparency to securing digital identities, the possibilities are vast. Blockchain can provide a foundational technology for building a new generation of transactional applications that establish trust, accountability, and transparency while streamlining business processes.

The path forward involves not only technological innovation but also strategic vision and leadership. Embracing blockchain technology requires a willingness to experiment and collaborate across sectors. It demands leaders who are not only technologically savvy but also capable of driving change and fostering an ecosystem where innovation thrives.

For enterprises aiming to stay at the forefront of digital transformation, exploring blockchain technology is not just an option—it's becoming a necessity. The businesses that recognize the strategic value of blockchain and are early to adopt and integrate can gain a significant competitive advantage. As we venture into an increasingly digital world, the potential of blockchain to transform industries and redefine how we transact is enormous.

As you consider the role of blockchain in your digital transformation journey, it's essential to approach it with a blend of curiosity, caution, and strategic foresight. Investments in blockchain technology should be deliberate, aiming not just for technological innovation, but for creating real business value. Understanding blockchain is the first step in unlocking its potential to drive digital transformation, enhance competitiveness, and pave the way for a new era of digital trust and transparency.

In conclusion, blockchain technology represents a pivotal shift in how we conceive of and execute digital transactions. Its implications for efficiency, security, and transparency offer a glimpse into a future where digital trust is paramount. For leaders and entrepreneurs willing to navigate its complexities and harness its potential, blockchain stands as a beacon of digital transformation and innovation. The journey of understanding and applying blockchain within your organization is both challenging and rewarding, leading toward a future where digital and physical worlds seamlessly converge in trust and efficiency.

Potential Business Applications and Challenges As we delve into the exploration of blockchain beyond the realm of cryptocurrency, we're at the cusp of witnessing an era where traditional business processes are being challenged and redefined. The fascination with blockchain is not just in its ability to secure financial transactions but in its potential to transform various aspects of business operations, from supply chain management to intellectual property rights enforcement. However, the path to integrating blockchain into business systems is fraught with both technical and organizational challenges that leaders must navigate.

Blockchain technology promises an unprecedented level of transparency, security, and efficiency in transactions. Imagine conducting business transactions without the need for a centralized authority to validate them. This autonomous approach could revolutionize industries by enabling smart contracts that automate and enforce agreements without human intervention. The implications for reducing operational costs and increasing transaction speed are profound. Nevertheless, the challenge lies in adopting a technology that necessitates a fundamental change in understanding traditional business models and transaction frameworks.

The application of blockchain in supply chain management exemplifies its potential to enhance traceability and accountability. Businesses can track the provenance and journey of products with accuracy and reliability, thereby significantly reducing the risks associated with counterfeiting and fraud. This level of transparency not only builds consumer trust but also streamlines regulatory compliance by providing a clear, immutable record of transactions. However, the integration of blockchain into existing supply chain systems demands substantial technical expertise and collaboration across all stakeholders, creating barriers to entry for many organizations.

Intellectual property rights protection is another promising application of blockchain. By creating tamper-proof digital ledgers, creators can securely register and track the usage of their intellectual property. This could deter infringement and ensure that creators receive fair compensation for their work. The challenge, however, lies in creating a universal framework that aligns with diverse legal systems and international intellectual property laws, making implementation complex.

Blockchain's potential in transforming healthcare records management is immense. By enabling secure, decentralized storage and sharing of medical records, blockchain can improve patient care and enhance privacy protection. Yet, the sensitivity and regulation of healthcare data present significant hurdles. Developing a blockchain solution that complies with global healthcare regulations, such as

HIPAA in the United States, while ensuring interoperability among different healthcare providers, requires meticulous planning and collaboration.

Financial services have been at the forefront of exploring blockchain technology. Beyond cryptocurrency, blockchain offers opportunities for streamlining payments, enhancing loan and credit systems, and improving the transparency of financial operations. However, the financial sector's stringent regulatory environment poses a significant challenge. Innovators must navigate a complex web of regulations that vary significantly by jurisdiction, complicating global implementation efforts.

The real estate sector stands to benefit from blockchain through the simplification of property transactions, title management, and record-keeping. By digitizing property titles and using smart contracts for transactions, blockchain can reduce fraud, speed up the conveyancing process, and lower transaction costs. Yet, the adoption of such a system requires overcoming entrenched interests of traditional stakeholders and updating legal frameworks to accommodate digital transactions.

Despite the potential benefits, the energy consumption associated with blockchain, particularly proof-of-work based systems, raises environmental concerns. Finding a balance between leveraging blockchain's capabilities and ensuring sustainability is a pressing challenge. Business leaders and technologists are exploring more energy-efficient consensus mechanisms such as proof-of-stake to mitigate these concerns.

Organizational resistance to change is another significant barrier. The shift to blockchain-enabled business models requires a cultural shift within organizations. Leaders must champion this transformation, fostering an environment that encourages innovation and experimentation. Convincing stakeholders of blockchain's long-term benefits, despite short-term disruptions and learning curves, is pivotal for successful adoption.

Interoperability between different blockchain platforms and legacy systems is critical for widespread adoption. Currently, the blockchain ecosystem is fragmented, with numerous platforms offering varying capabilities. Creating standards and protocols that enable seamless integration and communication between these systems is essential for businesses that wish to harness blockchain's full potential.

The knowledge gap poses yet another challenge. As a relatively new and rapidly evolving technology, there is a pressing need for education and training to equip current and future business leaders with the skills necessary to effectively implement and manage blockchain systems. Developing a workforce proficient in blockchain technology is critical for fostering innovation and staying competitive in the digital age.

Regulatory uncertainty also looms large over blockchain's potential applications. Governing bodies worldwide are still grappling with how to regulate blockchain technology effectively. Businesses eager to adopt blockchain must be prepared to navigate a shifting regulatory landscape, staying abreast of new laws and regulations that could impact their operations.

The security of blockchain networks, while robust, is not infallible. As the technology gains prominence, it becomes a more attractive target for cyberattacks. Strengthening the security of blockchain systems against increasingly sophisticated threats is a constant battle that requires ongoing attention and investment.

The scalability of blockchain technology is a concern for businesses looking to process high volumes of transactions rapidly. Current limitations in transaction processing speed and capacity can hinder the adoption of blockchain for applications requiring real-time processing. Efforts to enhance blockchain's scalability are ongoing, with solutions like layer two protocols emerging as promising approaches to address these challenges.

In conclusion, while the business applications of blockchain technology offer transformative possibilities, the journey towards widespread adoption is lined with challenges. Business leaders and entrepreneurs must approach these obstacles with a strategic mindset, viewing them not as insurmountable barriers but as opportunities to innovate and lead change. By actively engaging with the technological, organizational, and regulatory complexities of blockchain, businesses can unlock new value propositions and thrive in the digital age. The road ahead is challenging, yet it is paved with immense potential for those willing to navigate its twists and turns.

The Internet of Things (IoT): A Connected World

In the landscape of digital evolution, the Internet of Things (IoT) has emerged as a transformative force, ushering in a new era of connectivity that profoundly influences how businesses operate and interact with the world. Imagine a reality where every device, from the coffee machine in your office to the street lights illuminating our cities, is interconnected, providing real-time data to optimize operations, enhance customer experiences, and open new avenues for innovation. This connected world is not a distant future but a present reality, offering business leaders and entrepreneurs a unique opportunity to reimagine their operations and strategic directions. By harnessing the power of IoT, organizations can achieve unparalleled efficiency, agility, and customer intimacy. However, embracing IoT is more than just about technology; it's about envisioning a future where your business becomes a living ecosystem, responsive to the changing needs of the environment and society. As we delve deeper into the capabilities and potential of IoT, it's clear that those who can skillfully navigate this connected world will not only survive but thrive in the ever-evolving digital frontier. Therefore, understanding the intricacies of IoT and its impact on business models, customer engagement, and operational efficiency is imperative for any forward-thinking leader aiming to secure a competitive edge in the digital age.

How IoT is Transforming Business Operations As we journey deeper into the digital age, the Internet of Things (IoT) has emerged as a revolutionary force, transforming how businesses operate, innovate, and deliver value. At its core, IoT represents a vast network of interconnected devices, from the simplest sensors to the most complex machines, all communicating and sharing data. This interconnectedness provides unprecedented opportunities for businesses to streamline operations, enhance customer experiences, and create new revenue streams.

The transformative power of IoT lies not just in the ability to connect devices but in the way it enables businesses to harness data from these devices. This data, when analyzed and applied correctly, can lead to insightful decisions and strategic pivots that were previously unimaginable. For instance, predictive maintenance in manufacturing, powered by IoT, allows businesses to anticipate equipment failures before they occur, minimizing downtime and operational costs.

Moreover, IoT drives efficiencies across various business sectors. In logistics and supply chain management, for example, IoT technologies offer real-time tracking of goods and assets. This visibility helps in optimizing routes, reducing delays, and improving overall supply chain efficiency, directly impacting customer satisfaction and loyalty.

Customer experiences, too, are being redefined by IoT. Retailers are using IoT to personalize shopping experiences, using data gathered from in-store sensors and smart shelves to understand customer preferences and behaviors. This personalization, tailored to each individual's shopping habits and preferences, enhances customer engagement and fosters brand loyalty.

However, the benefits of IoT extend beyond operational efficiency and customer experience. IoT also plays a crucial role in enabling businesses to launch new products and services. With IoT, companies can gather detailed insights about how users interact with products, leading to better product designs and innovative features that meet the evolving needs of customers.

Energy management is another area where IoT is making significant inroads. Businesses are using IoT to monitor and control energy usage in real-time, leading to substantial cost savings and a reduced carbon footprint. This not only helps companies to be more sustainable but also aligns with the growing consumer demand for eco-friendly business practices.

The adoption of IoT technologies also facilitates safer workplaces. In industries such as construction and manufacturing, wearable IoT devices monitor worker health and safety, alerting them to potential hazards and ensuring that they are working under safe conditions.

While the benefits of IoT are vast, they don't come without challenges. Integrating IoT into existing systems requires substantial investment in technology and skills. Moreover, as businesses become more reliant on IoT devices, they also become more vulnerable to cybersecurity threats. Protecting the vast amounts of data generated by these devices is paramount.

To navigate these challenges, businesses must adopt a strategic approach to IoT implementation. This involves not only investing in the right technology and talent but also fostering a culture of innovation that embraces regulatory compliance, data privacy, and cybersecurity as foundational elements of IoT initiatives.

Furthermore, for IoT to truly transform business operations, it must be integrated with other digital technologies such as artificial intelligence (AI), blockchain, and cloud computing. AI, for instance, can amplify the benefits of IoT by providing advanced data analysis capabilities, while blockchain technology can offer secure and transparent ways to manage the vast amounts of data generated by IoT devices.

As IoT continues to evolve, it's clear that its impact on business operations is profound and far-reaching. Forward-thinking leaders are recognizing IoT's potential to not only improve efficiency and productivity but also to drive growth and innovation in an increasingly competitive and digital world.

The journey toward fully leveraging IoT is complex and requires a clear strategy, commitment, and adaptability. Businesses that successfully navigate this transformation stand to gain significant competitive advantages. They can not only expect to see improvements in operational efficiency and customer satisfaction but can also position themselves as innovators, leading the charge in the digital economy.

In conclusion, the IoT is not just reshaping business operations; it's redefining the possibilities of what businesses can achieve in the digital age. The convergence of IoT with other digital technologies is unlocking new opportunities, empowering businesses to deliver exceptional value, create meaningful customer experiences, and pave the way for sustainable growth and innovation. The key to unlocking this potential lies in embracing a holistic approach to digital transformation, one that intertwines technology integration with strategic foresight, cybersecurity, and a commitment to continuous improvement.

The transformative journey of IoT in business operations serves as a powerful reminder of the importance of digital innovation in today's business landscape. As companies continue to explore and harness the potential of IoT, the future of business operations looks not just interconnected but infinitely promising. The era of IoT-driven business transformation is here, and it's reimagining the fabric of industry and commerce in profound ways.

Security Challenges in an IoT-Driven World The march towards a world suffused with IoT devices brings with it a landscape lush with opportunities for innovation, operational efficiency, and enhanced customer experiences. However, this digital frontier is not without its challenges. Among the most pressing is the issue of security. In an IoT-driven world, the stakes for securing networks, devices, and data have never been higher.

The explosion of IoT devices has exponentially expanded the attack surface that businesses must defend. Every connected device, from smart thermostats in office buildings to industrial sensors in manufacturing plants, represents a potential entry point for malicious actors. The very interconnectedness that enables IoT devices to deliver value also makes them vulnerable to a variety of attacks, including data breaches, denial of service attacks, and even espionage.

Data privacy and protection are at the forefront of IoT security concerns. The vast amounts of data collected by IoT devices, while invaluable for driving business insights, also pose significant privacy risks if not properly secured. This data often includes sensitive personal information, making it a lucrative target for cybercriminals. Ensuring the integrity and confidentiality of this data thus becomes a paramount concern for businesses operating in an IoT-driven world.

Moreover, the complexity of IoT ecosystems presents a significant security challenge. These networks often span multiple jurisdictions, each with its own regulatory compliance requirements. Navigating this complex regulatory landscape, while ensuring that all components of the IoT ecosystem are secure, demands a robust and agile security strategy.

Another challenge lies in the heterogeneity of IoT devices and platforms. The myriad of manufacturers and service providers in the IoT space means a lack of standardization across devices and networks. This fragmentation creates vulnerabilities, as security solutions designed for one set of devices may be ineffective or even incompatible with others.

Addressing these security challenges requires a multifaceted approach. First and foremost, it demands adopting a security-by-design philosophy. Security must be integrated into the development lifecycle of IoT solutions, from the initial design phase through deployment and operation. This proactive stance ensures that security considerations are not an afterthought but a fundamental aspect of IoT development.

The role of encryption in safeguarding data cannot be overstated. By encrypting data both at rest and in transit, businesses can significantly reduce the risk of unauthorized access. However, encryption is just one piece of the puzzle. Comprehensive security measures must also include robust access controls, regular security assessments, and the deployment of security patches and updates.

Equally important is the cultivation of a security-aware culture within the organization. Employees should be educated on the best practices for IoT security, including the importance of strong passwords, recognizing phishing attacks, and the safe handling of data. This human element is often the weakest link in the security chain, and bolstering it can greatly enhance an organization's defense capabilities.

Collaboration is key to overcoming the security challenges of an IoT-driven world. This includes not only internal collaboration among IT, security, and operational teams but also external collaboration with device manufacturers, service providers, and regulatory bodies. By working together, stakeholders can share knowledge, develop best practices, and push for the adoption of security standards across the IoT ecosystem.

Emerging technologies also hold promise for IoT security. For instance, blockchain technology, with its decentralized and tamper-evident ledger, offers a potential solution for securing IoT networks and ensuring data integrity. Artificial intelligence and machine learning can enhance threat detection and response, enabling businesses to adapt to evolving security threats in real-time.

However, technology alone is not a panacea for IoT security challenges. A holistic approach that combines technology, processes, and people is essential for building resilience in an IoT-driven world. This includes developing incident response plans to mitigate the impact of security breaches and regularly evaluating and updating security measures to keep pace with evolving threats.

The journey towards securing an IoT-driven world is undeniably complex and fraught with challenges. Yet, it is also a necessary one. The benefits of IoT, from driving efficiency and innovation to enabling smarter decision-making and enhancing customer experiences, are too significant to ignore. By addressing the security challenges head-on, businesses can not only protect themselves against cyber threats but also unlock the full potential of IoT.

As we continue to navigate the digital frontier, the importance of IoT security will only grow. Businesses that prioritize security in their IoT initiatives will not only safeguard their operations and data but also gain a competitive edge in the digital economy. The task is daunting, but with the right strategies, technologies, and mindset, it is within reach.

In conclusion, the security challenges in an IoT-driven world demand our urgent attention and concerted effort. As business leaders and entrepreneurs, you have a critical role to play in shaping the future of IoT security. By embracing a proactive and collaborative approach, you can overcome these challenges and lead your organizations towards a secure, connected, and prosperous digital future.

Let this chapter serve as both a caution and an inspiration. The path ahead is fraught with challenges, but it is also lined with opportunities. The digital transformation journey is an ongoing process of learning, adapting, and innovating. In the realm of IoT security, as in all aspects of digital transformation, the potential for growth and positive change is limitless. Embrace the challenge, and let's build a secure and thriving digital future together.

Chapter 4:
Embracing Change: The Culture of Innovation

In a world where digital transformation is no longer a choice but a necessity, the creation and nurturing of a culture that embraces innovation is paramount. As leaders, fostering a digital mindset within your organization is not just about introducing new technologies but about inspiring your teams to reimagine the way they work and embrace the possibilities that come with change. This chapter delves into the critical aspects of building a foundation that supports and propels innovation, focusing on how to cultivate an environment that is not only ready but eager to adopt new digital practices. Overcoming resistance to change is a significant hurdle in this journey, yet, with the right strategies, it can be transformed into an opportunity for growth and learning. The essence of fostering a culture of innovation lies in empowering individuals, at all levels, to think creatively, challenge the status quo, and experiment without fear of failure. It's about showing how digital tools and processes can enhance efficiency, creativity, and connectivity, thereby creating value for the business and its customers. Embracing change is not merely about survival in the digital age; it's about thriving, leading, and setting new benchmarks in innovation and excellence.

Fostering a Digital Mindset

In the age of rapid digital transformation, developing a digital mindset is paramount for leaders and entrepreneurs. This mindset is the cornerstone of a culture that embraces change, innovation, and continual learning. It is not confined to the IT department but is a broad approach that should infuse every aspect of an organization's strategy and operations.

To foster a digital mindset, it's essential to understand its core components. At its heart, a digital mindset involves being customer-centric, agile, and data-driven. It requires a willingness to experiment and learn from both successes and failures. This adaptability is crucial in a landscape marked by fast-evolving consumer preferences and technological advancements.

Becoming customer-centric in a digital world means prioritizing the convenience, experience, and value your technology offerings bring to customers. Digital tools and platforms offer unprecedented opportunities to engage with customers directly and personalize their experiences. However, this requires a deep understanding of customer needs, behavior, and feedback, which can only be achieved through a culture that values and leverages data analytics.

Agility in a digital context goes beyond developing flexible business strategies. It involves adopting methodologies like Agile and Lean Startup in project management and product development. These methodologies emphasize rapid prototypes, iterative development, and responding to customer feedback, as opposed to following rigid plans and extensive upfront investments.

Being data-driven is non-negotiable in the digital age. Data analytics provide insights that can lead to better decision-making, enhanced customer experiences, and operational efficiencies. However, beyond merely collecting and analyzing data, a digital mindset requires a commitment to acting on these insights, even when they challenge conventional wisdom or require significant shifts in direction.

Fostering this mindset is not without challenges. It demands not only investment in technology and training but also a cultural shift that encourages innovation, risk-taking, and continuous learning. It's about creating an environment where employees at all levels are motivated to acquire digital skills and think in new ways.

Leaders play a crucial role in this transformation. They must exemplify the digital mindset, demonstrating openness to change, a commitment to data-driven decision-making, and a willingness to experiment and learn from failure. Furthermore, they need to champion digital initiatives and provide the necessary resources and support for their teams to innovate.

Implementing a digital mindset also requires rethinking organizational structures and processes. Traditional, hierarchical models can hinder the fast-paced decision-making and cross-functional collaboration that the digital age demands. Instead, empowering teams, flattening hierarchies, and fostering open communication can accelerate the adoption of digital initiatives.

Another key aspect is leveraging partnerships and ecosystems. In today's interconnected world, no organization can excel in all facets of digital technology alone. Building relationships with startups, academia, and even competitors can provide access to new ideas, technologies, and talent.

Embedding a digital mindset also means embracing digital ethics and responsibility. As businesses collect and utilize vast amounts of personal data, they must prioritize safeguarding privacy and ensuring the ethical use of technology. This not only helps in building trust with customers but also sets a solid foundation for sustainable growth.

Continuous learning and development are vital. The digital landscape is constantly evolving, and so are the skills needed to navigate it. Investing in ongoing education and development, from digital literacy programs to advanced technological training, ensures that everyone in the organization can contribute to and benefit from digital initiatives.

However, fostering a digital mindset is not an overnight endeavor. It's a strategic journey that involves reevaluating and often rebuilding the very core of the organization's DNA. It demands patience, persistence, and resilience from leaders and their teams.

Success stories of digital transformation often highlight the importance of vision, courage, and an unyielding drive to innovate. These organizations didn't just adopt new technologies; they reshaped their cultures, strategies, and value propositions around the digital mindset.

As we move forward, the difference between thriving and merely surviving in this digital era will increasingly hinge on an organization's ability to foster this mindset. It is what will empower businesses to leverage digital innovations, anticipate and lead market shifts, and create unprecedented value for their customers and stakeholders.

In conclusion, fostering a digital mindset is the linchpin of navigating the digital frontier successfully. It embodies a holistic approach to embracing technological advancements, where driving digital transformation becomes a shared vision that permeates every level of the organization. It's this shared vision that will enable forward-thinking leaders and entrepreneurs to not only withstand the tides of digital disruption but to ride them to new heights of innovation and success.

Overcoming Resistance to Change

Change, particularly in the digital age, is the only constant. Yet, in the journey of transforming a business to thrive amidst digital disruption, leaders often face a significant hurdle: resistance to change. This resistance can stem from a myriad of reasons——fear, uncertainty, or even a lack of awareness about the benefits that change can bring. Overcoming this resistance is crucial for fostering a culture of innovation that not only embraces but also drives forward digital transformation.

Understanding the root causes of resistance is the first step towards addressing it. Often, employees fear that they might not possess the skills required in a digitally transformed workplace or worry about job security in the face of automation and artificial intelligence. On the other hand, some leaders might resist change due to a deep-seated attachment to traditional ways of running the business that have brought success in the past.

Communicating the vision behind the digital transformation is essential. It's not just about implementing new technologies but about creating a new way of working that leverages these technologies to drive growth, efficiency, and enhance customer experience. Leaders must articulate this vision clearly and repeatedly, highlighting not only the business benefits but also how the change will positively impact the workforce.

Building a digital mindset across the organization is another critical aspect. This involves training and educating employees on digital technologies and trends, showing them how these tools can streamline operations, and even enrich their own work. By demystifying technology, you can alleviate fears and build a more confident and tech-savvy workforce.

Engagement and participation are powerful strategies in overcoming resistance. Involve employees in the transformation process, giving them a sense of ownership and control over the changes happening around them. This could be through pilot projects, ideation sessions, or digital literacy workshops. When people are part of the change, they are more likely to support and advance it.

Rewarding and recognizing early adopters and champions of change within the organization can also set a positive precedent. When their peers see them succeed and even thrive with new technologies and processes, it can motivate others to follow suit. This approach helps create internal influencers who can drive change from within the ranks.

Leadership is pivotal in driving any major change, including digital transformation. Leaders themselves must embody the change they wish to see, demonstrating a commitment to learning and using digital tools. Their enthusiasm for and investment in the change process can inspire the rest of the organization to embrace the journey.

Addressing the human aspect of digital transformation is as important as the technological one. Providing support systems, whether through mentorship programs, digital transformation task forces, or emotional support resources, can help employees navigate the changes more comfortably. This support reassures them that they're not alone in this journey and that the organization is invested in their success and well-being.

Creating a culture of continuous learning and innovation is crucial. In a world where digital technologies evolve at a breakneck pace, fostering an environment that encourages ongoing education, experimentation, and even failure, can make adaptability a core organizational strength.

Leaders must cultivate resilience within the organization. Change can be daunting, and setbacks are part of any transformation journey. Encouraging a mindset that views challenges as opportunities for growth and learning can make the journey more palatable and even exciting for the entire team.

Ensuring transparency throughout the transformation process can help in managing expectations and reducing fears. Share both the successes and the challenges openly, and discuss the next steps and strategies for overcoming any obstacles. This level of honesty fosters trust and strengthens the team's commitment to the shared vision.

Aligning individual goals with the broader vision of digital transformation can make the change more meaningful for everyone involved. When employees see how their work contributes to the organization's success and innovation, they're more likely to take an active role in driving change.

Flexibility and adaptability are key. The path of digital transformation is rarely a straight line. Being open to course corrections, listening to feedback, and being willing to adjust plans as needed can help in navigating the complexities of change more effectively.

Finally, patience is vital. Transformation doesn't happen overnight. It's a gradual process that requires persistence, commitment, and a long-term vision. Celebrating small wins along the way can keep the momentum going and remind everyone of the progress being made.

Overcoming resistance to change for a culture of innovation requires a multifaceted approach that addresses both the human and technological aspects of transformation. By leading with empathy, vision, and resilience, businesses can navigate the uncertainties of digital disruption and emerge stronger, more agile, and ready for the future.

Chapter 5:
Digital Strategy and Leadership

In the heart of digital transformation lies the crucial role of crafting a compelling digital strategy, underscored by visionary leadership. This journey begins with defining a digital roadmap that aligns with your organization's overarching goals, ensuring that every technological investment and innovation moves you closer to your strategic objectives. The essence of digital strategy is not just about adopting technology, but about rethinking business models, processes, and customer interactions in the digital age. It's about making deliberate choices on where to play and how to win, leveraging digital technologies to gain competitive advantage.

Leadership, however, is the linchpin in this transformative endeavor. It's the driving force that champions the change, navigates through uncertainties, and inspires the organization to embrace a digital-first mindset. Leaders must be catalysts, fostering an environment that encourages experimentation, agile learning, and the continuous iteration of digital solutions. They need to embody the digital vision, demonstrating an unwavering commitment to steering the organization through its digital voyage. This demands a blend of strategic foresight, digital literacy, and the adaptability to lead by example in the rapidly evolving digital landscape.

Effective digital leadership goes beyond merely managing technology initiatives; it's about cultivating a culture that is receptive to change, innovation, and constant learning. Leaders must bridge the gap between the traditional and digital realms, ensuring seamless integration and harmony between diverse teams and technologies. They are tasked with empowering their teams, breaking down silos, and building a cohesive, digitally savvy workforce that thrives on collaboration and innovation.

In essence, the journey of digital transformation is as much about technology as it is about people and culture. It requires a balanced approach that intertwines digital strategy with impactful leadership. Together, they set the stage for businesses to not only survive but flourish in the digital era. As we delve deeper into the nuances of defining your digital roadmap and the pivotal role of leadership in digital transformation, remember that the crux of success lies in envisioning the digital future, inspiring your team to embark on this journey with you, and relentlessly pursuing your strategic goals with passion and perseverance.

Defining Your Digital Roadmap

In the journey toward digital transformation, embarking on the path without a map can lead to wandering in an ever-evolving landscape of technology and market shifts. The cornerstone of navigating this journey successfully is to define your digital roadmap meticulously, a strategic blueprint that guides your organization from its current state to a future where it thrives in the digital era. Crafting such a roadmap demands a deep understanding of where you are, where you need to go, and the steps necessary to get there.

First, it's essential to assess your organization's digital maturity. This involves a comprehensive look at your current technologies, processes, culture, and customer interactions. Understanding where you stand on this spectrum enables you to identify the gaps and opportunities for digital optimization and innovation. It's not just about the technology but how your business model aligns with digital capabilities to deliver value.

Next, envisioning the future state of your organization under the lens of digital possibilities is vital. This isn't merely projecting current trends but imagining how your industry could be reshaped by emerging technologies and changes in consumer behavior. It's about asking, 'What if?' and daring to envisage a future that sets you apart in the digital marketplace.

Setting clear, actionable goals is the next step in your roadmap. These objectives should be ambitious yet achievable, pushing your organization forward without straying into the realms of wishful thinking. They ought to be tied closely to the overall business strategy, ensuring that digital transformation efforts are squarely aimed at driving growth, enhancing customer experience, or achieving operational excellence.

With goals in place, the planning phase moves to identifying the digital initiatives that will help you achieve these targets. This is where strategic consideration of technology investments, talent acquisition, and process changes comes into play. It's about prioritizing projects that offer the most value and align with your company's strategic direction, ensuring resources are allocated efficiently.

Crucial to the roadmap is a timeline that lays out when and how these digital initiatives will be rolled out. This timeline must be realistic, providing enough time for implementation, learning, and iteration. It should include milestones that mark significant achievements in the journey and help keep the transformation on track.

The success of a digital roadmap also hinges on its flexibility. The digital landscape is perpetually in flux, with new technologies emerging and consumer preferences shifting. Your roadmap should be adaptable, ready to pivot in response to these changes without losing sight of the overarching goals.

Leadership commitment is another critical element. Transforming an organization digitally is not the sole responsibility of the IT department; it requires buy-in and active participation from leadership at all levels. Leaders must champion the digital vision, mobilizing resources and driving the cultural shift necessary for transformation.

Communication plays a pivotal role throughout the digital transformation journey. It's imperative to keep all stakeholders informed and engaged, from employees to customers. Transparent communication about the goals, process, and progress of the digital roadmap helps in building trust and fostering a culture of innovation.

Measurement and analysis are integral to steering the digital transformation effectively. Establishing Key Performance Indicators (KPIs) related to your digital initiatives allows you to monitor their impact and make data-driven adjustments to your strategy. This feedback loop is crucial for continuous improvement and achieving the desired outcomes.

Risks and challenges are inevitable in any transformational journey. Proactively identifying potential roadblocks and devising mitigation strategies ensure that the roadmap remains viable. Whether it's technological hurdles, resistance to change, or market dynamics, foreseeing these challenges enables your organization to navigate them more adeptly.

Aligning your digital transformation with customer needs ensures that your efforts result in enhanced value for those you serve. It's about leveraging digital to meet and exceed customer expectations, thereby fostering loyalty and driving growth. This customer-centric approach is a key differentiator in the digital age.

Securing the necessary resources for your digital transformation journey is also crucial. This encompasses not just the financial investment but also sourcing the right talent and technology. Having the right mix of skills and tools at your disposal can significantly accelerate your progress on the digital roadmap.

Last but not least, cultivating a culture of digital innovation is paramount. This means more than just adopting new technologies; it involves embracing a mindset that encourages experimentation, learning from failures, and continuously pushing the boundaries of what's possible. A culture that supports innovation is the bedrock upon which digital transformation can thrive.

In conclusion, defining your digital roadmap is a complex yet rewarding process that requires thoughtful planning, steadfast leadership, and an unwavering focus on delivering value through digital means. It's about setting a vision, charting a course, and navigating your organization through the challenges and opportunities of the digital age with agility and purpose. As you embark on this journey, remember that the roadmap is not set in stone but a living document that evolves with your organization and the digital landscape. By staying adaptable, committed, and customer-focused, you can lead your organization to new heights in the era of digital transformation.

The Role of Leadership in Digital Transformation

Leadership in the digital age is not just about guiding a company through its current challenges but also about anticipating and adapting to the future. The cornerstone of successful digital transformation lies in visionary leadership—a blend of foresight, strategy, and the ability to ignite change within the organization. A leader's role in this transformative journey cannot be overstated. It is they who set the tone and pace for digital adoption and innovation.

In the realms of digital transformation, leaders are tasked with crafting a vision that marries technology with business goals. This vision serves as a guiding light for the organization, keeping all efforts aligned and focused on the most impactful outcomes. The true test of leadership is not just in creating this vision but in communicating it effectively, ensuring that every member of the team not only understands it but is also fully engaged in bringing it to life.

Moreover, the digital landscape is rife with complexities and rapid changes. Here, leaders must exhibit agility—being prepared to pivot strategies, re-evaluate investments in technologies, and embrace innovative business models when necessary. Such agility allows organizations to stay relevant and competitive in a fast-evolving digital marketplace.

Empowerment is another critical aspect of leadership in digital transformation. Leaders must empower their teams by fostering a culture of innovation where new ideas are encouraged, and failure is seen as a stepping stone to success. This involves providing the team with the resources, training, and support needed to experiment and innovate while ensuring a safe environment where risks can be taken without fear of retribution.

Collaboration is key in a digitally-transforming world. Leaders must break down silos and encourage cross-functional teams to work together on digital initiatives. This approach not only leverages diverse perspectives for better solutions but also fosters a culture of unity and shared purpose. Collaboration across different levels of the organization also helps in the seamless adoption and integration of digital technologies.

The importance of continuous learning in leadership cannot be overlooked. In a landscape defined by rapid technological advancements, leaders must be perpetual learners to stay ahead. This means not just keeping abreast of the latest digital trends and technologies but also understanding the wider implications of these advancements on their industry, business model, and competitive landscape.

Leaders must also champion customer-centricity. Digital transformation often revolves around enhancing the customer experience. Leaders should instill a mindset within the organization that prioritizes understanding and meeting customer needs through innovative digital solutions. This customer-first approach ensures that digital initiatives are always aligned with creating value for the customer, thus driving customer loyalty and business growth.

Transparency and open communication are pivotal during digital transformation. Change can be unsettling, and the shift towards digital operations is no exception. Leaders must maintain an open dialog with their teams, addressing concerns, sharing progress, and celebrating milestones. This transparency not only helps in managing the change but also in building trust and commitment among team members.

Prudent risk management is a vital leadership trait in navigating digital transformation. While innovation requires taking risks, leaders must ensure that these are calculated risks. This involves thorough due diligence, scenario planning, and having solid risk mitigation strategies in place. By managing risk effectively, leaders can foster a culture of smart innovation.

The democratization of innovation is a notable shift in organizations undergoing digital transformation. Leaders should encourage innovation at all levels, recognizing that great ideas can come from anywhere within the organization. By democratizing innovation, leaders can harness a wider pool of ideas, increase engagement, and accelerate the pace of digital transformation.

Moreover, integrity and ethical leadership are paramount. As businesses increasingly rely on digital technologies and data, leaders must uphold the highest standards of ethics and data privacy. This not only builds trust with customers and stakeholders but also sets a strong foundation for sustainable growth in the digital era.

Leadership in digital transformation also involves nurturing the next generation of leaders. This ensures the sustainability of the transformation efforts and cultivates a leadership pipeline that is well-versed in digital innovation and agile methodologies. By mentoring and developing talent, leaders can ensure that the organization remains on the cutting edge of digital transformation.

In the end, the role of leadership in digital transformation is a multifaceted one. It is about being a visionary, a strategist, a communicator, an innovator, and an ethical guardian. Leaders must navigate the complexities of the digital landscape with a clear vision, an agile approach, and a commitment to continuous improvement and innovation. By embodying these qualities, leaders can guide their organizations through the transformative journey, unlocking new opportunities and driving sustainable growth in the digital age.

As we continue to delve deeper into the intricacies of digital strategy and leadership, it becomes clear that the role of a leader is not static but ever-evolving. The digital age demands leaders who are not only attuned to the current technological advancements but are also forward-thinking, ready to lead their organizations into the future with confidence and resilience. The successful leaders of tomorrow are those who embrace change, champion innovation, and lead with integrity, ensuring that their organizations not only survive but thrive in the digital age.

Chapter 6:
Reinventing Customer Experience in the Digital Age

In an era where the digital landscape is constantly evolving, the reinvention of customer experience stands as a pivotal chapter in the journey of digital transformation. The digital age beckons a seismic shift in how businesses interact with their customers, moving beyond traditional service paradigms to create more personalized, engaging experiences. Enabling this transformation are the pillars of data analytics and technology, which together, unlock opportunities for unprecedented levels of personalization and engagement. By harnessing the power of data analytics, businesses can glean insightful customer preferences and behaviors, paving the way for tailored experiences that resonate on a deeper level. Technology amplifies this connection, introducing platforms and tools that enrich interactions and simplify customer journeys. From AI-driven recommendations to immersive digital environments, the digital age offers a canvas for businesses to innovate their approach to customer service. This chapter discusses how leading-edge companies are leveraging these capabilities to set new standards in customer satisfaction, fostering loyalty and driving growth in the process. The essence of reinventing customer experience lies not just in adopting new tools but in embedding a customer-centric culture that thrives on innovation and adaptability, ensuring businesses remain relevant in the eyes of the digital-savvy consumer.

Using Data Analytics for Personalization

In an era where digital transformation sets the stage for business success, the art of personalization has emerged as a cornerstone of customer experience. Data analytics, with its ability to sift through vast amounts of information and derive meaningful insights, is at the heart of this new frontier. This section delves into how businesses can leverage data analytics to tailor experiences, products, and services to meet the ever-evolving expectations of their customers.

The journey of personalization through data analytics begins with understanding your customer. Today, every digital interaction a customer has with your brand offers data points that, when analyzed effectively, can reveal comprehensive insights about their preferences, behaviors, and needs. It's not just about collecting data, but about interpreting it to construct a detailed customer profile.

Moreover, personalization is not merely recommending products based on past purchases. It's an intricate dance of presenting the right message, at the right time, through the right channel. Data analytics empowers businesses to predict customer needs, sometimes even before the customer realizes them. This anticipatory service can enhance customer satisfaction and loyalty significantly.

The integration of machine learning algorithms with data analytics has been a game-changer for personalization. These algorithms can learn from each interaction, constantly improving the accuracy of recommendations and decisions. It's a dynamic process that continually refines the customer experience, making it more personal and relevant with each interaction.

Yet, harnessing the power of data analytics for personalization demands a robust data infrastructure. Businesses must invest in technology platforms that can collect, store, and analyze data efficiently. It's equally important to ensure data quality and integrity, as the decisions made based on this data directly impact the customer experience.

Data privacy and security are paramount considerations in this context. With the increase in data breaches and stringent data protection regulations, businesses must tread carefully. They need to strike a balance between personalization and privacy, ensuring they have consent to use data and are transparent about how it's being used.

Implementing personalization through data analytics also calls for a cross-functional approach. It requires collaboration across departments – from IT and marketing to sales and customer service. Each team brings unique insights that contribute to a unified view of the customer, enabling more accurate and effective personalization.

Measurement and analytics go hand in hand when it comes to personalization. Establishing key performance indicators (KPIs) for personalization efforts is crucial. These metrics can help track the effectiveness of personalized experiences in driving desired customer behaviors, such as increased engagement, conversion rates, and customer loyalty.

A critical aspect of personalization is the willingness to experiment and learn. A/B testing, for example, can provide valuable feedback on what personalization tactics work best. This iterative process fosters a culture of continuous improvement, ensuring that personalization strategies remain aligned with customer expectations and business objectives.

The potential of data analytics for personalization extends beyond marketing and sales. It can enhance customer support by predicting issues and facilitating proactive solutions. Additionally, product development can benefit from insights into customer needs and preferences, guiding the creation of offerings that better meet market demands.

Adopting a customer-centric mindset is fundamental to succeeding with personalization. It involves moving away from product-focused strategies and towards a deep understanding of the customer's journey. This shift is critical in identifying moments where personalized interactions can have the greatest impact on customer experience.

As we navigate the digital age, personalization will continue to evolve. Emerging technologies like artificial intelligence, blockchain, and the Internet of Things (IoT) present new opportunities for creating deeply personalized experiences. Businesses ready to explore and integrate these technologies will stay ahead in the race to win customer hearts and minds.

However, the path to personalization excellence is fraught with challenges. It requires a steadfast commitment to data-driven decision-making, a willingness to embrace technological advancements, and a culture that values customer-centricity above all. Yet, the rewards of achieving superior personalization through data analytics are immense, offering a competitive edge that is hard to replicate.

In conclusion, the imperative for businesses today is clear – to reinvent customer experience through personalization powered by data analytics. It's a strategic investment that goes beyond technology and data. It's about cultivating a deep understanding of your customers and delivering value that resonates on a personal level. As business leaders and entrepreneurs, your ability to harness the power of personalization will define your success in the digital age. Let the data be your guide, your creativity the path, and your commitment to customer satisfaction the driving force behind your efforts.

The journey of personalization is an ongoing one, with each step forward opening new doors to connect with your customers in meaningful ways. In leveraging data analytics for personalization, you're not just transforming customer experience; you're setting the stage for lasting relationships that fuel business growth. It's an exciting time to be at the helm of digital transformation, steering your organization toward a future where personalized customer experiences are not just expected but cherished.

Enhancing Customer Engagement through Technology

In the rapidly evolving digital landscape, customer engagement has emerged as a critical battleground for businesses aiming to thrive. The touchstone for success is no longer just the quality of products or services but how effectively a business can engage, understand, and meet the ever-changing expectations of its customers. This chapter delves into the myriad ways technology can be harnessed to deepen customer engagement, offering tangible strategies to transform passive interactions into dynamic, meaningful connections.

At the heart of enhancing customer engagement lies the adept use of data analytics. In today's digital age, every click, like, share, and comment is a goldmine of insights into what customers care about. Forward-thinking businesses leverage this data to craft personalized experiences that resonate on a personal level with their audience. It's not about bombarding customers with content, but curating experiences that speak directly to their needs and preferences.

Artificial intelligence (AI) and machine learning algorithms offer unparalleled capabilities in this regard. By analyzing vast datasets, AI can predict customer behavior, automate personalized communication, and even foresee needs before the customer articulates them. Take, for example, chatbots. These AI-powered conversational agents can provide 24/7 support, answering queries, offering recommendations, and assisting with purchases, thus ensuring a seamless and interactive customer experience.

The Internet of Things (IoT) further expands the horizon of possibilities for customer engagement. IoT devices collect and exchange data in real-time, offering a holistic view of the customer journey across different touchpoints. Businesses can leverage this information to anticipate needs, tailor services, and even adjust the product offering in real-time, creating a highly responsive and interactive customer environment.

Mobile technology, too, plays a pivotal role. The ubiquity of smartphones has opened up new avenues for engagement. Optimizing websites and applications for mobile users, employing geolocation services to offer timely, location-based promotions, and leveraging QR codes and AR for interactive marketing campaigns are just a few examples of how mobile technology can enhance customer interaction.

Social media platforms serve as powerful tools for building communities and fostering interactive customer relationships. They allow businesses to listen actively to their audience, engage in two-way conversations, and nurture a loyal customer base. Innovative use of social media, from live streams to user-generated content and beyond, can significantly amplify engagement and create a sense of belonging among customers.

Email marketing, though often considered traditional, remains an effective tool when powered by technology. Automated, personalized emails based on customer behavior and preferences can generate significant engagement. This strategy hinges on delivering value, not volume, ensuring that each communication is tailored to the recipient's specific interests and stage in the customer journey.

Augmented Reality (AR) and Virtual Reality (VR) are redefining interactive experiences, enabling customers to explore products and services in immersive, engaging ways. Whether it's trying on clothes virtually, visualizing furniture in a room, or experiencing a travel destination in VR before booking, these technologies are transforming how customers interact with brands.

Gamification is another innovative approach, infusing the customer experience with elements of play, competition, and rewards. By making engagement fun, businesses can encourage desired behaviors, deepen loyalty, and create vibrant, interactive platforms for customers to explore.

Blockchain technology, while often associated with cryptocurrencies, has significant implications for customer engagement. Its applications in ensuring data integrity, securing transactions, and enabling transparent loyalty programs can help build trust and deepen customer relationships.

However, technology alone is not a silver bullet. The human element remains crucial. Emphasizing empathy, understanding, and genuine connection in every technological interaction ensures that the engagement feels personal and meaningful. Combining technological innovation with a deep-seated customer-centric approach is where true engagement magic happens.

Overcoming the challenges of implementing these technological solutions requires a strategic approach. It starts with a clear understanding of the business objectives, the target audience, and what engagement means in the context of your industry. It also necessitates investment in the right technology and training for your team to effectively deploy these tools.

Measurement and analytics play a critical role in refining engagement strategies. By establishing clear metrics for engagement, businesses can track the effectiveness of different technologies and approaches, learn from insights, and continuously optimize for better results.

The future of customer engagement is undeniably digital. As technologies continue to evolve, so too will the ways in which businesses can interact with and engage their customers. Staying ahead of the curve requires not just adopting new technologies, but constantly reimagining the customer experience in innovative, interactive, and meaningful ways.

In conclusion, enhancing customer engagement through technology is a journey of continuous innovation and adaptation. It's about leveraging the right mix of data analytics, AI, IoT, mobile technology, social media, AR, VR, and other digital tools to create deeply personalized and engaging customer experiences. By doing so, businesses not only meet the evolving expectations of their digital-savvy customers but set themselves apart in a competitive digital landscape. The future belongs to those who can transform customer interactions into immersive, value-driven experiences - and the time to start is now.

Chapter 7:
Digital Marketing and Branding

In an era where technology perpetually reshapes the landscape of how businesses connect with their customers, leaders poised at the helm of this digital revolution understand that mastery over digital marketing and branding isn't just advantageous—it's essential. The digital domain extends far beyond mere presence; it is a realm where brand narratives are woven into the daily lives of consumers, leveraging every click, every view, and every interaction to forge deeper connections. This chapter delves into the metamorphosis of marketing in the digital sphere, exploring how tools and platforms that seemed nascent yesterday are today's battlegrounds for brand loyalty and consumer engagement. You'll discover the artistry behind engaging content strategies that do more than just sell—they tell a story, your story, in ways that resonate universally. As you navigate through the subtleties of social media dynamics, you'll grasp how to harness its power to not only reach your audience but to truly connect with them, turning participants into partners in your brand's ongoing narrative. The digital age demands nothing short of reinvention, urging you to rethink not just how you market, but more fundamentally, how you envision your brand's place in the digital panorama. Embrace this journey through digital marketing and branding not as a challenge to surmount but as the most thrilling opportunity to redefine and assert your brand's significance in the digital age.

The Evolution of Digital Marketing

The landscape of digital marketing has undergone a significant transformation since its inception. From the rudimentary banner ads of the early internet days to the sophisticated AI-driven campaigns we see today, the journey reflects a broader digital evolution. This evolution is not merely technological but cultural, influencing how brands communicate with their audiences and how consumers perceive and interact with brands.

In the nascent stages of the internet, digital marketing was an extension of traditional marketing, merely transposing existing strategies into a new digital format. Email marketing campaigns, basic online advertisements, and rudimentary websites became the pioneers of this era, setting the stage for what was to come. These efforts, while innovative at the time, barely scratched the surface of what digital marketing would become.

As the internet became more integrated into daily life, social media emerged as a powerful tool for brands to reach out to their target audiences. Platforms like Facebook, Twitter, and Instagram allowed businesses to craft more personal and engaging narratives. This era highlighted the shift from one-way communication, where brands spoke at consumers, to a more interactive dialogue, fostering a sense of community and loyalty.

Simultaneously, the rise of search engines like Google revolutionized how information was accessed online. Search engine optimization (SEO) and pay-per-click (PPC) advertising became essential strategies for increasing visibility and driving traffic to websites. This period underscored the importance of being readily discoverable by consumers actively seeking information, products, or services online.

The introduction of smartphones and mobile internet access further accelerated the digital marketing evolution. Mobile marketing, responsive web design, and location-based advertising started to gain prominence. Brands recognized the need to reach consumers not just online but wherever they were, in ways that were tailored to the unique context of mobile usage.

Content marketing also began to take center stage, driven by the understanding that consumers sought valuable, relevant content rather than outright sales pitches. Brands became publishers, investing in blogs, videos, infographics, and podcasts to engage audiences. This strategy helped companies establish thought leadership, build trust, and deepen customer relationships over time.

As digital platforms became more sophisticated, the data generated by user interactions grew exponentially. This wealth of data allowed marketers to gain deeper insights into consumer behavior, preferences, and patterns. Big data analytics and customer relationship management (CRM) systems became pivotal in crafting personalized marketing strategies, enhancing the ability to tailor messages and offers to individual consumers.

The advent of artificial intelligence and machine learning has marked the latest phase of digital marketing's evolution. AI technologies enable unprecedented levels of personalization, automating the delivery of content and offers based on real-time analysis of consumer behavior. Chatbots, personalized recommendations, and predictive analytics are just a few examples of how AI is being leveraged to create more engaging and effective marketing campaigns.

Moreover, the concept of omnichannel marketing has emerged, recognizing that consumers interact with brands across multiple platforms and devices. Creating a seamless experience across all these touchpoints has become crucial for brands looking to maintain relevance and cohesion in their messaging. This approach ensures that whether a consumer engages with a brand through social media, a mobile app, or in-store, their experience is consistent and integrated.

The evolution of digital marketing is also characterized by an increased focus on measurement and accountability. With advanced analytics tools, marketers can now accurately track the performance of their campaigns, measure return on investment (ROI), and make data-driven decisions to optimize strategies in real time. This focus on performance metrics has shifted the marketing paradigm from a cost center to a revenue generator.

In the realm of social media, influencer marketing has brought about a significant change in how brands connect with their audiences. Leveraging the credibility and reach of influencers, brands can tap into established communities, engender trust, and drive engagement in a way that traditional advertising cannot.

Privacy and personalization have become two sides of the same coin in the digital age. As consumers become more concerned about how their data is used, brands are challenged to balance personalized marketing efforts with respect for privacy and data protection. This dynamic has led to the development of more transparent data practices and the rise of consent-based marketing.

The future of digital marketing lies in the continued fusion of technology, creativity, and data analytics. Emerging technologies like augmented reality (AR), virtual reality (VR), and the Internet of Things (IoT) promise to open new avenues for creative and immersive brand experiences. These will likely redefine consumer expectations and the ways in which marketers engage their audiences.

As we look ahead, the importance of storytelling remains at the heart of digital marketing. The tools and platforms will continue to evolve, but the goal remains the same: to connect with consumers in meaningful ways. Brands that can harness the power of digital to tell compelling stories, build communities, and deliver value will thrive in the ever-changing digital landscape.

The evolution of digital marketing is a testament to the broader digital transformation that has swept across all facets of business and society. For forward-thinking business leaders and entrepreneurs, understanding this evolution is crucial. It not only offers insights into how marketing has changed but also provides a blueprint for navigating the digital age. In this journey, agility, innovation, and a commitment to understanding the consumer are key. By embracing the digital marketing evolution, businesses can unlock new opportunities, foster deeper connections with their customers, and ultimately, drive sustained growth in an increasingly digital world.

Leveraging Social Media and Content Strategy

In the current digital era, the importance of a robust social media and content strategy cannot be overstated. As part of a comprehensive approach to digital marketing and branding, these elements serve not only as vessels for communication but as fundamental tools for building and nurturing brand identity, engaging with customers, and driving business objectives. The fluid, dynamic nature of digital platforms means the strategies we adopt must be equally adaptable and forward-thinking.

The core of a successful social media strategy hinges on understanding your audience. Knowing who they are, what they care about, and how they interact with the digital world allows for the creation of content that resonates and engages. It's not just about broadcasting messages but fostering conversations and building relationships. This two-way communication channel significantly enhances customer engagement and loyalty.

Content strategy, meanwhile, goes hand in hand with social media. At its heart, content is the fuel for your digital marketing engine. Whether it's blog posts, videos, infographics, or podcasts, compelling content is what draws your audience in and keeps them coming back. More than ever, quality trumps quantity. In a world awash with information, outstanding, valuable content sets your brand apart.

Integration is another crucial concept in leveraging social media and content strategy effectively. Your digital presence can't be segmented into silos. Instead, it should be a coherent ecosystem where each part complements and amplifies the others. This means aligning your content across all platforms, ensuring consistency in messaging, and using each channel's strengths to your advantage.

Analytics play a pivotal role in refining social media and content strategies. By analyzing data on how users interact with your content and social media posts, you gain invaluable insights into what works and what doesn't. This data-driven approach allows for constant optimization, ensuring your strategies remain effective and aligned with your audience's evolving preferences.

Personalization is another key area. Today's consumers expect experiences tailored to them. Leveraging data analytics, artificial intelligence, and machine learning can help create personalized content experiences at scale. This not only boosts engagement but also strengthens the bond between your brand and its customers.

To stay ahead of the curve, it's essential to keep an eye on emerging trends and technologies. Social media platforms evolve rapidly, and what's effective today may be obsolete tomorrow. Staying informed and being ready to pivot your strategy in response to new developments is critical for sustained success.

User-generated content is a powerful asset that can amplify your brand's message and authenticity. Encouraging your audience to share their own stories and experiences related to your brand can foster a sense of community and trust that's hard to achieve through traditional marketing alone.

Authenticity and transparency have become more than buzzwords; they are the cornerstones of successful digital branding. Consumers seek real connections with brands. Showcasing the human side of your business, admitting to mistakes, and being open about your processes and challenges resonate with today's audiences and foster trust.

Storytelling is an age-old technique that has found new life in digital marketing. A compelling story can captivate an audience, evoke emotions, and drive engagement in ways that factual presentations of information simply cannot match. Integrating storytelling into your content strategy can elevate your brand and create memorable experiences.

Collaborations and partnerships can extend the reach of your social media and content efforts. By aligning with influencers, thought leaders, or other brands that share your values, you can tap into their audiences, bringing fresh perspectives and added credibility to your brand.

Finally, it's critical to remember the human element in digital marketing. Technology is a tool, not the end goal. The aim is to connect with people, understand their needs, and provide value. This human-centric approach should be at the heart of your social media and content strategy, guiding every decision and action.

In conclusion, leveraging social media and content strategy is not simply about keeping up with trends or using the latest technologies. It's about creating genuine connections, providing value, and continuously adapting to the changing digital landscape. By understanding your audience, producing quality content, and using data to inform your strategies, you can achieve outstanding results and drive your business forward in the digital age.

As you move forward, keep innovation, adaptation, and engagement as your guiding principles. The digital frontier is vast, and the opportunities for those willing to explore and leverage it are limitless. Your journey in leveraging social media and content strategy is just the beginning of tapping into the full potential of digital marketing and branding.

Embrace the challenges and opportunities of the digital transformation with an open mind and a proactive stance. The future belongs to those who are ready to innovate, adapt, and connect in the ever-changing digital landscape. Your commitment to leveraging social media and content strategy is pivotal to navigating this journey successfully.

Chapter 8:
The Future of Work:
Digital Workplaces and Workforce

In the heart of digital transformation lies the future of work, a realm where digital workplaces and workforces thrive amidst the rapid pace of technological evolution. At its core, creating a flexible and collaborative digital workplace is not just an operational change but a strategic imperative that positions organizations to leapfrog into future opportunities. The metamorphosis into digital spheres demands a reimagination of how work is conducted, where physical boundaries are transcended, and collaboration tools become the lifelines of productivity. As leaders, the onus is on us to sculpt an environment that not only embraces these changes but also nurtures a culture of innovation and agility.

Yet, the journey doesn't end at crafting digital spaces; it extends to preparing the workforce for this seismic shift. The essence of empowering a digital-ready workforce lies in fostering digital literacy, nurturing continuous learning, and cultivating an adaptability mindset. This transition presents a unique opportunity to redefine roles, pave paths for upskilling, and unlock human potential like never before. By harnessing the power of digital tools and platforms, we can propel our teams towards unparalleled efficiency, creativity, and innovation. In navigating the future of work, our mission is clear: to lead with vision, drive transformative change, and wield the digital revolution as our catalyst for unlocking a future brimming with potential and possibilities.

Creating a Flexible and Collaborative Digital Workplace

In the realm of digital transformation, the concept of work and how it's accomplished has undergone a seismic shift. The cornerstone of this evolution is the creation of a flexible and collaborative digital workplace. Crafting such an environment isn't just about integrating the latest technologies; it's about reimagining the very essence of collaboration and flexibility in a work setting. This section delves into the pivotal elements that define a digital workplace and outlines strategies to foster a culture that embraces these dimensions.

At its core, a digital workplace leverages technology to improve work processes, engage employees, and foster a culture of innovation. It's an environment that supports a myriad of working styles, encourages open communication, and facilitates seamless collaboration, irrespective of physical locations. The drive towards digital workplaces is propelled by the increasing demand for a work-life balance, the globalization of business operations, and the need to attract talent in a competitive landscape.

To initiate the shift towards a more digital-centric work environment, leaders must first understand that technology alone isn't the panacea. It's the synergy between technology, people, and processes that creates a truly flexible and collaborative digital workplace. This involves deploying tools that not only enhance productivity but also promote an inclusive culture where every voice can be heard and valued.

Collaboration tools like Slack, Microsoft Teams, and Zoom have become the linchpins of digital communication, enabling teams to connect and collaborate in real-time, regardless of geographic barriers.

But the adoption of these tools should be complemented with policies that encourage their effective use. For instance, establishing guidelines for video meetings can ensure that these interactions are as productive and inclusive as possible.

Flexibility in the digital workplace goes beyond the ability to work from any location; it encompasses when the work is done. Implementing flexible working hours can contribute significantly to employees' overall well-being and job satisfaction. This approach recognizes that peak productivity times vary among individuals and that work can often be done outside the traditional 9-to-5 framework.

Data security and privacy are paramount in a digital workplace. As the boundaries between professional and personal life blur with remote work, companies must adopt robust cybersecurity measures to protect sensitive information. This means regular audits, employing end-to-end encryption for communications, and educating employees on security best practices.

Creating a culture that supports learning and development is another critical aspect of a digital workplace. With the rapid pace of technological change, continuous learning opportunities can help employees keep up with new tools and methodologies. This could be in the form of online courses, webinars, or learning modules integrated within the collaborative platforms themselves.

Leadership plays a pivotal role in driving the transition to a digital workplace. Leaders must embody the change they wish to see, leveraging digital tools for communication and decision-making processes. This sets a precedent for the rest of the organization and demonstrates the practical benefits of adopting new ways of working.

Feedback mechanisms are essential to identify bottlenecks and areas for improvement in a digital workplace. Regular surveys, suggestion boxes, or digital forums can provide employees with a channel to voice their concerns and suggestions. This feedback can then be used to refine strategies and tools to better meet the needs of the workforce.

In addition to the internal benefits, a digital workplace can significantly enhance customer experiences. By utilizing digital channels for customer interactions and leveraging data analytics for personalized services, companies can provide superior customer service, thereby driving customer satisfaction and loyalty.

However, the transition to a digital workplace is not without its challenges. Resistance to change, data privacy concerns, and the digital divide are issues that businesses may encounter. Overcoming these obstacles requires a thoughtful approach that addresses the concerns of all stakeholders and facilitates a smooth transition.

Moreover, as businesses forge ahead in their digital workplace journeys, they must remain vigilant about maintaining a balance between productivity and employee well-being. The allure of always-on connectivity can lead to burnout if not managed properly. Encouraging digital detoxes and setting boundaries for work time can help in creating a more sustainable work environment.

The future of work is unequivocally digital. As businesses continue to navigate the complexities of digital transformation, creating a flexible and collaborative digital workplace is not just an option; it's a necessity. This evolution requires a holistic approach that encompasses technology, culture, and leadership. By doing so, businesses can harness the full potential of their workforce, drive innovation, and secure a competitive edge in the digital age.

In conclusion, the journey towards a digital workplace is an ongoing process that demands continuous adaptation and evolution. By embracing this shift, businesses can create an environment that not only meets the demands of the modern workforce but also paves the way for future growth and success in an increasingly digital world.

As we move forward, the principles of flexibility, collaboration, and innovation will remain the guiding stars for organizations aiming to thrive in the digital era. The digital workplace is more than a trend; it's the foundation of a future where work is not a place you go, but something you do—efficiently, effectively, and enthusiastically.

Preparing the Workforce for Digital Transformation

The dawn of digital transformation has ushered in a new era for the workplace and its workforce. As businesses pivot toward more digitally centric models, the imperative to prepare the workforce for this shift becomes not just necessary but critical to success. The journey toward digital transformation demands more than just the adoption of new technologies; it necessitates a comprehensive re-skilling and up-skilling of the workforce.

At the heart of preparing the workforce for digital transformation is the development of a digital mindset. This mindset recognizes the value of agility, continuous learning, and adaptability in navigating the digital landscape. Workers today must be equipped not only with technical skills but also with the ability to think critically and solve complex problems in a digital context.

Digital literacy is no longer a complimentary skill—it's a fundamental requirement. This literacy transcends familiarity with basic digital tools and encompasses an understanding of data analytics, cybersecurity, and digital ethics. As such, training programs must evolve beyond traditional learning models to incorporate digital proficiencies that align with the future of work.

The role of leadership in this transformation is indispensable. Leaders must champion a culture of innovation and learning, creating an environment where experimentation is encouraged, and failure is seen as a step toward advancement. By modeling a commitment to digital fluency, leaders can inspire their teams to embrace the challenges of digital transformation.

Collaboration across different sectors of the business is also key to effective digital transformation. By breaking down silos and fostering interdisciplinary teams, companies can leverage a wide range of perspectives and skills, leading to more innovative solutions and a more cohesive digital strategy.

To support this shift, companies should also leverage mentoring and coaching. Experienced professionals can share invaluable insights with their less experienced colleagues, not only in using new digital tools but also in applying them effectively within their specific job roles.

Continuous learning platforms play a critical role in keeping the workforce up-to-date with the latest technologies and methodologies. These platforms should be accessible, engaging, and capable of delivering personalized learning experiences to meet the diverse needs of the workforce.

The concept of a lifelong learner has never been more relevant. In the face of rapid technological developments, the capacity to learn and adapt continuously is perhaps the most valuable skill any worker can possess. Organizations need to cultivate this capacity, offering opportunities for growth that extend well into an employee's career.

Data literacy is another critical area for workforce development. In a world driven by data, the ability to interpret and leverage information is essential. Training in data analysis, visualization, and decision-making should be integral to preparing the workforce for the challenges ahead.

Moreover, the rise of AI and automation presents both opportunities and challenges. Rather than viewing these technologies as a threat to employment, they should be seen as tools that can augment human capabilities. Workers should be trained on how to integrate these technologies into their daily workflows, thus enhancing efficiency and innovation.

The shift to digital also demands a new approach to performance management. Traditional metrics and evaluation methods may not suffice in the digital age. Instead, performance management systems need to reflect the value of innovation, collaboration, and digital project execution.

Embracing diversity and inclusivity is another crucial element. Diverse teams bring a range of perspectives that are invaluable in solving complex digital problems. An inclusive culture not only attracts a broader talent pool but also fosters a more creative and innovative workspace.

Lastly, the psychological aspect of digital transformation should not be underestimated. Change can be daunting, and the shift to a digital-first workplace may induce anxiety among employees. Support structures, including counseling and stress management resources, should be made available to help employees navigate these changes.

Preparing the workforce for digital transformation is an ongoing process that mirrors the continual evolution of technology itself. It requires a holistic approach that encompasses skill development, leadership, culture, and well-being. By investing in their workforce, companies are not just adapting to the present; they are preparing to lead in the future.

In conclusion, as we stand at the brink of widespread digital transformation, the readiness of the workforce is as much about cultivating a digital culture as it is about technical skills. The businesses that will thrive are those that recognize and act on the imperative to foster a digitally fluent workforce, ready to navigate the complexities and seize the opportunities of the digital age.

Chapter 9:
Navigating the Ethical and Legal Implications

As we delve into the vast ocean that is digital transformation, it's imperative to navigate the treacherous waters of ethical and legal frameworks thoughtfully. In today's rapidly evolving digital landscape, the lines between right and wrong, lawful and unlawful can often seem blurred. It's not just about leveraging cutting-edge technologies to reimagine your business processes or enhance customer experiences, but about doing so in a manner that respects privacy, prioritizes security, and adheres to an ever-growing tapestry of regulations. This chapter challenges you to ponder on how your business actions affect stakeholders, and it serves as a compass to guide you through the complex ethical dilemmas and compliance issues that accompany digital innovations. Ethical considerations like data privacy and AI ethics are not mere checkboxes on your corporate compliance list; they are the very foundation upon which sustainable and socially responsible business practices are built. Similarly, understanding the nuances of regulations, such as GDPR in Europe or CCPA in California, isn't just about avoiding fines; it's about winning and maintaining the trust of your customers in a world where trust is both exceedingly valuable and increasingly rare. As leaders steering the ship of change, it's your responsibility to ensure that your voyage into digital transformation is marked not only by the innovations you adopt but by the principled way in which you implement them, proving that your business doesn't just operate within the letter of the law but embodies the spirit of ethical integrity.

Privacy, Security, and Ethical Considerations

In the heart of digital transformation lies not just the awe-inspiring potential of technology to reshape our world, but also the profound responsibility to navigate its challenges with integrity and foresight. As business leaders, we're not just architects of the future; we're custodians of the values that define us. In the throes of innovation, privacy, security, and ethical considerations must serve as our compass, guiding us through murky waters.

Privacy is more than a compliance issue; it's a covenant with our customers. In an era where data is as valuable as currency, how we collect, store, and use this information speaks volumes about our corporate ethos. It's not just about adhering to regulations like GDPR or CCPA, but about fostering trust. When customers share their data with us, they're entrusting us with a part of their identity. Betraying that trust not only damages our reputation but diminishes the very fabric of digital society.

Security, in its essence, is the bedrock upon which digital enterprises must be built. The sophistication of cyber threats evolves in lockstep with technological advancements. As leaders, it's imperative that we invest not only in robust cybersecurity frameworks but also in a culture of awareness and vigilance. A breach can have far-reaching consequences, from financial loss to irreparable harm to our brand's integrity. It's a reminder that in the digital realm, vigilance must be unwavering.

Ethical considerations in technology are increasingly coming to the fore as AI and machine learning become ubiquitous in business applications. The algorithms powering these innovations must be scrutinized for bias, fairness, and accountability. It's a stark reminder that behind every dataset and algorithm lies human lives and decision-making. We must ensure that these technologies are implemented in ways that augment human potential without infringing on rights or exacerbating inequalities.

The intersection of AI and privacy presents a peculiar paradox. While AI can unlock unprecedented insights and efficiencies, it also raises critical questions about consent and the ethical use of data. Navigating this landscape requires a nuanced understanding of both technology and the moral imperatives at stake. It calls for transparent algorithms, ethical data sourcing, and continuous dialogue with stakeholders about the implications of AI-driven decisions.

The IoT brings connectivity and convenience but also introduces new vulnerabilities. Every connected device is a potential entry point for cyber threats. Securing an IoT ecosystem is a complex endeavor that goes beyond traditional cybersecurity measures. It demands a holistic approach that encompasses device security, data protection, and network integrity. As leaders, we must champion the development of secure IoT frameworks that safeguard not just data, but also the operational continuity of our businesses.

Blockchain technology promises a new frontier of transparency and security, especially in transactions and supply chains. However, it also poses ethical considerations related to energy consumption and regulatory oversight. Embracing blockchain requires a balanced approach, one that harnesses its potential while being cognizant of its footprint and the need for governance mechanisms that ensure ethical usage.

As we forge ahead, regulatory challenges in the digital era will only intensify. Compliance is a moving target, with regulations evolving as fast as the technologies prompting them. Staying ahead means being proactive, not just reactive. It means embedding privacy and security into the DNA of our products and services, ensuring that they are not just market-ready, but ethically sound and regulation-compliant.

But beyond compliance lies a broader ethical responsibility. The digital divide is widening, and we have a role in bridging it. Access to technology is not just about connectivity; it's about ensuring that the benefits of digital transformation are universally equitable. This means creating inclusive products, championing digital literacy, and working to mitigate the socio-economic disruptions that technology can sometimes precipitate.

Transparency is key in all these endeavors. It's about demystifying our use of data and technology for our customers, creating clear channels of communication, and being open about both our successes and our failures. This openness builds trust and fosters a culture of accountability, both within our organizations and in the broader ecosystem.

The path forward demands a collaborative effort. No single entity has all the answers, and the complexities of digital transformation require a multi-stakeholder approach. This means working with peers, governments, regulators, and civil society to shape an environment that nurtures innovation while safeguarding ethical standards and societal values.

Continuous learning is also vital. The landscape of digital transformation is perpetually shifting, and staying informed is crucial. As leaders, we must cultivate a culture of curiosity and lifelong learning within our organizations, encouraging our teams to embrace change and the challenges it brings.

In conclusion, as we navigate the ethical and legal implications of digital transformation, we're reminded that technology is a tool, and how we wield it reflects our values. Privacy, security, and ethical considerations are not just checkboxes on a compliance list; they are expressions of our commitment to doing business in a way that benefits not just our bottom line, but society at large.

Let's embrace this journey not just with the ambition to succeed but with a resolve to do so responsibly. The choices we make today will define the legacy we leave for future generations. In this digital age, let's be remembered not just for the innovations we create, but for the trust we build and the ethical standards we uphold.

As we stand on the brink of a new era, let's take a moment to reflect on the magnitude of our responsibility. It's an opportunity to redefine what success looks like in the digital age—an age where profitability and ethical responsibility are not mutually exclusive but are interwoven into the very fabric of our business models. The journey of digital transformation is as much about leading with integrity as it is about embracing innovation.

Regulatory Challenges in the Digital Era

In the journey through digital transformation, businesses encounter myriad challenges, not least among them the complex web of regulatory challenges that accompany the digital era. As technologies like AI, blockchain, and IoT reshape industries, they also bring to the fore new legal conundrums and ethical considerations. This section dives deep into the labyrinth of regulatory issues confronting businesses today, offering insights into navigating this terrain with finesse.

The pace at which technology evolves invariably outstrips the speed of regulatory response. Legislators and regulators often find themselves playing catch-up with innovations, leading to a regulatory landscape that can seem labyrinthine and disjointed. For business leaders, this presents a unique challenge: how to innovate responsibly, ensuring compliance with current regulations while anticipating future legal shifts.

The first step in navigating regulatory challenges is understanding the nature of digital data and its implications for privacy. In an age where data is the new currency, guarding customer privacy becomes not just a legal requirement but a cornerstone of trust. Regulations such as the General Data Protection Regulation (GDPR) in Europe and various privacy laws in the United States highlight the global shift towards stringent data protection measures. These laws set the framework for how businesses should collect, store, and use personal information, mandating a transparent approach to data handling.

However, compliance is not merely about avoiding penalties; it's about building a culture of privacy that aligns with your business values. Implementing robust data protection measures not only safeguards against legal risks but also enhances brand reputation and customer trust. The question then becomes, how can businesses effectively balance the drive for innovation with the need for compliance?

A key strategy is staying abreast of regulatory changes and understanding their implications for your business. This requires a proactive approach, wherein legal and compliance teams are not siloed but integrated into the strategic planning process. By embedding regulatory awareness into every stage of product and service development, businesses can avoid the pitfalls of non-compliance and leverage compliance as a competitive advantage.

Another significant regulatory challenge in the digital era is the ethical use of artificial intelligence. As AI systems become more pervasive in business operations, questions arise about accountability, bias, and transparency. Regulators are increasingly focusing on creating frameworks that ensure AI is used ethically, pushing businesses to consider not just what they can do with AI, but what they should do. This involves implementing principles such as explainability, fairness, and accountability into AI systems, ensuring they operate within ethical boundaries and societal norms.

The complexity of regulating technologies like blockchain and IoT further complicates the regulatory landscape. These technologies offer tremendous potential for creating efficiencies and new business models but come with their own set of regulatory hurdles. For instance, blockchain's decentralization challenges traditional notions of regulatory oversight, while IoT's interconnectedness raises significant security and privacy concerns.

Addressing these challenges requires a multifaceted approach. Collaboration between industries and regulators can lead to the development of standards and guidelines that foster innovation while protecting public interests. Additionally, leveraging regulatory technology (RegTech) solutions can help businesses manage compliance more efficiently, automating the tracking of regulatory changes and compliance processes.

Globalization adds another layer of complexity to the regulatory challenges of the digital era. As businesses operate across borders, they must navigate a mosaic of jurisdictions, each with its own regulatory requirements. This necessitates a nuanced understanding of international laws and the ability to adapt business practices to varying legal landscapes. The key is adopting a global compliance strategy that can be localized to meet specific regulatory requirements.

Emerging technologies will inevitably continue to push the boundaries of regulation. In anticipation, forward-thinking business leaders must foster a culture of compliance that is nimble, informed, and integrated into the DNA of the organization. This involves ongoing education, continuous risk assessment, and open dialogue with regulatory bodies.

The digital era brings into sharp relief the tension between innovation and regulation. Yet, this should not be viewed as a barrier but as an opportunity to innovate responsibly. By embracing regulatory challenges as a catalyst for positive change, businesses can navigate the digital landscape with agility and integrity.

Ultimately, the goal is to achieve a balance where innovation flourishes within a framework of robust regulatory standards. This balance is not static but an evolving equilibrium that requires vigilance, adaptability, and a commitment to ethical principles. Businesses that can successfully navigate this balance will not only thrive in the digital era but will also lead the way in shaping the future of their industries.

In conclusion, the regulatory challenges of the digital era are formidable but not insurmountable. With a strategic approach that prioritizes ethical considerations, compliance, and collaboration, businesses can turn regulatory hurdles into opportunities for innovation and trust-building. As the digital landscape continues to evolve, so too will the regulatory frameworks that govern it. Staying ahead of these changes, and indeed, helping to shape them, is the hallmark of true digital leadership.

Chapter 10:
Case Studies: Success
Stories of Digital Transformation

In the heart of this digital transformation journey, where theory meets practice, lies a collection of powerful narratives that stand as beacons of insight and inspiration for forward-thinking leaders. This chapter delves into an array of case studies that not only demonstrate the monumental successes of digital transformation across various industries but also the resilience, innovation, and strategic foresight that propelled these organizations into new dimensions of operational excellence and market dominance. From startups that have disrupted century-old industries with groundbreaking digital business models to traditional enterprises that have reinvented themselves in the face of digital upheaval, these stories encapsulate the essence of transformative success. They offer a unique lens through which we can examine the practical applications of digital strategies that were discussed in previous chapters, illustrating how embracing technological advances, fostering an innovative culture, and leveraging data analytics can culminate in unparalleled competitive advantages. As we dissect these success stories, we'll uncover the key lessons learned from leading digital innovators and reveal how these insights can be strategically applied to your business to navigate the complexities of digital transformation. The journey of each organization featured in this chapter not only serves as a testament to the power of digital innovation but also as a guidebook for any leader aspiring to chart a successful course through the digital frontier.

Lessons Learned from Leading Digital Innovators

As we delve into case studies of digital transformation success stories, we uncover a treasure trove of insights and strategies that have propelled businesses to the forefront of innovation. These pioneers in digital transformation have not only navigated the complexities of change but have mastered the art of thriving in a digitally dominated landscape. Their journeys offer invaluable lessons for any business leader or entrepreneur aiming to carve out a successful path in the digital era.

The first lesson is the critical importance of a clear vision. Successful digital innovators have a concise understanding of where they want their digital transformation journey to take them. This vision goes beyond mere technology adoption; it encompasses a complete overhaul of processes, culture, and customer engagement strategies. It's about envisioning a future where digital is at the heart of all operations and making that vision a reality through steadfast commitment and strategic planning.

Agility and the willingness to adapt are also key hallmarks of successful digital innovation. The digital landscape is perpetually evolving, with new technologies emerging at a breakneck pace. Leaders in this space are those who remain nimble, ready to pivot their strategies in response to new trends and technologies. They understand that what worked yesterday may not work tomorrow, and they're always prepared to iterate and evolve.

Another critical factor is the embrace of a culture of innovation. This requires fostering an environment where experimentation is encouraged, and failure is seen not as a setback but as a step forward. Leading digital innovators understand that innovation is not just about technology; it's about people and their ability to think creatively, work collaboratively, and approach problems with fresh perspectives. They invest in building teams that are diverse, curious, and empowered to take risks.

Customer-centricity lies at the heart of all successful digital transformations. These leading innovators pay close attention to their customers' needs, preferences, and behaviors, using insights gathered from data analytics to tailor their offerings and personalize experiences. They recognize that in a digital world, customers have more choices than ever, and capturing their loyalty requires going above and beyond to deliver value and convenience.

The strategic use of data is another lesson gleaned from these success stories. Data is the lifeblood of digital innovation, providing the insights necessary for making informed decisions, optimizing operations, and creating personalized customer experiences. Leaders in digital transformation don't just collect data; they harness its power, using analytics to uncover trends, predict customer behavior, and drive growth.

Collaboration and partnerships are often critical components of a successful digital strategy. Innovators understand that they can't do everything alone and that building ecosystems of partners can provide the complementary skills, technologies, and market access needed to accelerate their transformation efforts. They seek out strategic alliances that can help them enter new markets, develop new products or services, or enhance their technological capabilities.

Investing in talent and skills development is also a common thread among these innovators. As the demand for digital skills continues to outpace supply, leading firms are proactive in developing the capabilities of their workforce. They invest in training and development programs, bring in external expertise when needed, and foster a culture of continuous learning and improvement.

Foresight and investment in emerging technologies before they hit the mainstream have also set apart the true pioneers of digital innovation. These leaders are not afraid to explore emerging technologies such as AI, blockchain, or IoT, understanding that early experimentation can lead to significant competitive advantages down the line.

Perhaps most importantly, successful digital transformation requires strong leadership. Leaders who have steered their organizations through successful digital revolutions share a few key traits: vision, determination, and the ability to inspire and motivate their teams. They are not just managers; they are visionary leaders who can rally their organizations around a shared goal of digital excellence.

Attention to ethical considerations and regulatory compliance has also been a hallmark of successful digital innovators. In an era where data breaches and privacy concerns are rampant, these leaders have built trust with their customers by prioritizing data security, privacy, and ethical use of technology. They understand that in the digital age, trust is an invaluable currency.

Digital transformation is not just about technology; it's also about change management. Leading innovators recognize that technology alone cannot drive change without the right mindset, culture, and processes in place. They focus on managing the human side of digital transformation, ensuring that their people are engaged, motivated, and equipped to navigate the shift.

Successful digital innovators also understand the importance of scalability. They design their digital initiatives with an eye toward future growth, ensuring that their infrastructure, processes, and business models can accommodate expansion without losing pace or efficiency.

Finally, persistence is key. Digital transformation is not an overnight process; it requires time, effort, and unwavering dedication. The most successful digital leaders are those who persist through the inevitable challenges and setbacks, remaining focused on their long-term vision for transformation.

As we reflect on these lessons from leading digital innovators, it becomes clear that success in digital transformation is multifaceted. It requires vision, agility, a culture of innovation, customer-centricity, strategic use of data, partnerships, investment in talent, foresight in technology adoption, strong leadership, ethical considerations, effective change management, scalability, and persistence. For business leaders and entrepreneurs seeking to navigate the challenges of digital transformation, these insights offer a blueprint for success in the digital age.

How to Apply These Insights to Your Business

In the journey of digital transformation, understanding the successes of others is a guiding light. But illumination alone won't clear the path; it's the steps you take that ultimately define the journey. To translate the lessons from our case studies into tangible outcomes for your business, it's necessary to embrace a multifaceted approach, blending strategy with action, and vision with pragmatism.

First and foremost, identify your digital transformation objectives. What exactly are you aiming to achieve? Increased operational efficiency? Enhanced customer experience? Or perhaps, breaking into new markets with digital products? Clarity on objectives will not only define your trajectory but also help in communicating the vision to your team, thereby aligning efforts across the board.

Assess your current digital maturity. Take a realistic stock of where your business stands in terms of digital capabilities. This involves evaluating your technological infrastructure, digital skills within your team, and existing digital processes. Understanding your starting point is crucial for mapping out a digital transformation journey that is both ambitious and achievable.

Leverage data as your compass. Data analytics can provide invaluable insights into customer behavior, operational bottlenecks, and untapped market opportunities. In the stories of digital transformation, data-driven decision-making emerges as a common thread among successful companies. It's not just about collecting data, but rather about interpreting it effectively to guide strategic decisions.

Invest in digital skills and culture. Digital transformation is as much about technology as it is about people. Fostering a digital culture and investing in skills development are indispensable. Encourage a mindset of continuous learning and experimentation. Remember, a workforce that is comfortable with digital technologies and adaptive to change is your biggest asset in this journey.

Address resistance to change head-on. Change management is a critical component of digital transformation. It's natural for resistance to surface, but how you manage it can make all the difference. Communication is key - articulate the 'why' behind the change, involve teams in the transformation process, and celebrate milestones to generate momentum.

Choose your technologies wisely. Not every cutting-edge technology is a fit for your business. Evaluate technologies based on their relevance to your objectives, their integration capabilities with your existing systems, and the skills required to maintain them. It's about selecting tools that offer both immediate benefits and the potential for long-term value.

Prioritize customer experience in your digital initiatives. In a world where customer expectations are constantly evolving, delivering a seamless digital experience can be a competitive differentiator. This means not just digitizing existing services, but reimagining them from a customer-centric perspective.

Embrace agile methodologies. The digital landscape changes at a blistering pace, necessitating agility in how projects are managed and executed. Agile methodologies prioritize flexibility, continuous improvement, and rapid iteration, allowing businesses to adapt quickly to emerging trends and customer feedback.

Experiment and iterate. Successful digital transformation is often the result of experimentation. Not every initiative will be a home run, and that's okay. The key is to iterate quickly - launch small-scale pilots, gather feedback, refine your approach, and scale up successful experiments. This lean approach reduces risks and accelerates learning.

Strengthen your cybersecurity posture. As you deepen your digital footprint, ensuring the security of your data and digital assets becomes paramount. A breach can not only have financial ramifications but can also erode trust in your brand. Adopting a proactive stance towards cybersecurity, with regular audits and updates, is imperative.

Build strategic partnerships. In the digital domain, ecosystems can offer leverage that individual efforts cannot. Collaborating with technology providers, industry peers, and even startups can open up new avenues for innovation and growth. Strategic partnerships can also help you navigate areas outside your core expertise.

Measure and refine your digital transformation strategy. Establish clear metrics for success and regularly review your progress. This entails not just tracking operational metrics, but also gauging customer satisfaction and employee engagement in the context of digital transformation. Be prepared to pivot your strategy based on what the data tells you.

Finally, cultivate patience and resilience. Digital transformation is not an overnight endeavor; it's a strategic, long-term commitment. Setbacks are part of the process, but they also offer opportunities for learning and refinement. Stay focused on your vision, be adaptable, and maintain unwavering belief in the transformative potential of digital technologies.

Applying the insights from successful digital transformations to your business is a journey of discovery, adaptation, and perseverance. By embracing the strategies outlined above, you are not merely surviving in the digital age but positioning your business to thrive and lead. The future belongs to those who are ready to harness the digital wave, turning challenges into opportunities for innovation and growth.

Chapter 11:
Looking Ahead: The Next
Wave of Digital Disruption

As we stand on the brink of a new era, the digital landscape continues its relentless advance, reshaping the horizon of business and innovation. This next wave of digital disruption isn't just looming on the horizon; it's crashing over us, demanding agility, foresight, and the courage to dive into uncharted waters. Emerging technologies are at the heart of this transformation, poised to redefine competitiveness, operational efficiency, and customer experience. For forward-thinking leaders, the focus now shifts to not just navigating but mastering these turbulent changes. Preparing your business for future digital shifts is paramount, entailing a holistic approach that embraces adaptability, fosters continuous learning, and cultivates an ecosystem ripe for innovation. The key is not to view this wave as a looming challenge but as a spectrum of unparalleled opportunities, ready to unlock new value streams, drive growth, and catalyze a renaissance of entrepreneurial ingenuity. In this chapter, we'll explore the strategic imperatives that will equip you to harness the potential of emerging technologies and position your enterprise at the forefront of the digital frontier, where the only constant is change, and the capacity to innovate becomes the most valuable currency.

Emerging Technologies to Watch

As we stride further into the future, the pace at which technology evolves seems to accelerate, transforming how we live, work, and conduct business. Within this whirlwind of change, certain emerging technologies stand out, not only for their innovativeness but also for their potential to disrupt the current paradigms. These technologies promise to redefine industries, reshape consumer expectations, and rewrite the rules of competition.

First on our watch list is **quantum computing**. Far from being a figment of science fiction, quantum computing is making strides towards practical application. Its profound computing power, capable of solving complex problems much quicker than current supercomputers, heralds a new era of innovation. From drug discovery to optimizing logistics, the ramifications for business are immense. Savvy leaders are already exploring partnerships and investments in this space, recognizing its potential to redefine industry landscapes.

Another critical area is **augmented reality (AR) and virtual reality (VR)**. These technologies are steadily transitioning from gaming and entertainment to become powerful tools for businesses. AR and VR offer immersive experiences that can revolutionize training and education, enhance design and creativity, and offer new ways to engage with customers. Their ability to merge digital information with the physical world opens up a realm of possibilities for creating value in ways we're just beginning to comprehend.

5G technology is another pivotal innovation. While its predecessor, 4G, brought us the mobile internet, 5G promises to be exponentially faster and more reliable, enabling a surge in IoT applications and smart devices everywhere. This leap in connectivity will facilitate innovations such as autonomous vehicles, smart cities, and advanced telemedicine applications, compelling businesses to reevaluate their operations and customer service offerings.

We can't discuss emerging tech without mentioning **edge computing**. As data generation from IoT devices grows, relying solely on centralized data processing becomes untenable. Edge computing addresses this by processing data closer to where it's collected, reducing latency and bandwidth use. This change lays the groundwork for real-time analytics and decision-making, essential for applications requiring immediate responses, such as in manufacturing and emergency services.

In parallel, **biotechnology** is advancing at a breathtaking pace, spurred by recent global health challenges. Crispr technology, gene editing, and synthetic biology are part of this wave, offering potential cures for diseases and efficient, sustainable approaches to food production. While the ethical implications are profound, the opportunities for positive impact are equally significant.

The rise of **generative artificial intelligence (AI)** marks a significant evolution in how AI is used in creative and coding processes. This technology can design software, create content, and even generate art, setting the stage for new forms of creativity and innovation while challenging our notions of authorship and originality.

The field of **cybersecurity**, too, is evolving rapidly. With the digitization of almost every aspect of business, cyber threats are becoming more sophisticated. Emerging technologies in cybersecurity, such as AI-driven threat detection and blockchain for secure transactions, are critical for protecting data integrity and maintaining customer trust.

In the realm of **sustainability**, technology plays a key role in addressing environmental challenges. Innovations in clean tech, green energy, and sustainable materials are not just ethical imperatives but offer competitive advantages as consumers increasingly favor environmentally conscious companies.

The concept of **digital twins**—virtual replicas of physical objects or systems—provides unprecedented opportunities in product development, predictive maintenance, and decision-making processes. By simulating real-world conditions, businesses can test scenarios and optimize operations without the risks and costs associated with physical trials.

Furthermore, the **decentralization of finance** through technologies like blockchain is creating alternatives to traditional financial systems. Cryptocurrencies, decentralized finance (DeFi), and non-fungible tokens (NFTs) challenge conventional banking and investment models, pushing leaders to rethink financial transactions' security and efficiency.

As we consider the tapestry of emerging technologies, it's clear that adaptability is key. The ability to pivot and embrace new opportunities will define the successful leaders and companies of tomorrow. Encouraging a culture of innovation, continuous learning, and openness to change is foundational to navigating this rapidly evolving landscape.

Moreover, while these technologies offer incredible potential, they also present challenges. Ethical considerations, privacy concerns, and the need for regulatory frameworks are among the hurdles that need careful navigation. Engaging with these technologies responsibly, with a focus on creating value for society, will be a hallmark of leading businesses in the digital age.

In conclusion, the future is brimming with technological possibilities that promise to enrich our lives and propel businesses into new dimensions of success. By staying informed and agile, leaders can harness these emerging technologies to foster growth, inspire innovation, and achieve sustainable competitive advantages. The next wave of digital disruption is on the horizon, and the time to prepare is now. The only question that remains is: Are you ready to seize the opportunities it brings?

Embracing these emerging technologies requires foresight, courage, and strategic agility. As we explore the vistas of the future, the potential for innovation is limitless. The journey ahead is challenging, but for those willing to lead the charge, it is undeniably exciting. Let's stride forward together, shaping a future that leverages technology for the betterment of all.

Preparing Your Business for Future Digital Shifts

In an era where digital advancements are occurring at an exponential rate, it's imperative that businesses not only keep pace but also anticipate and prepare for future shifts. The landscape of digital transformation is vast and ever-evolving, requiring a proactive and strategic approach. As leaders, the ability to navigate through these changes and leverage them for growth can set your business apart in a competitive ecosystem.

The first step in preparing for these digital shifts is embracing a culture of continuous learning and adaptability. The rapid pace of technological change means that what's cutting-edge today might become obsolete tomorrow. Encouraging an organizational culture that values staying informed about technological trends and flexible in adopting new practices is crucial. This not only involves regularly updating your team's skills but also fostering an environment where innovation is nurtured and rewarded.

Understanding the breadth of digital technologies and their potential impact on your industry is another pivotal aspect. From AI and machine learning to blockchain and IoT, each of these technologies holds the power to revolutionize business operations, customer engagement, and market strategies. Conducting thorough research and analysis to discern which technologies align with your business goals will enable you to focus your efforts and resources more effectively.

The third strategy involves developing a digital-first mindset throughout your organization. This means prioritizing digital solutions in problem-solving, operations, and customer interactions. A digital-first approach is not solely about technology adoption; it's about transforming your business model to better meet the demands of a digital economy. This requires a shift in thinking at all levels of the organization, from the executive team down to frontline employees.

Next, invest in data analytics and cybersecurity. Data is the lifeblood of digital transformation, providing insights that can drive decision-making and innovation. However, the value of data is tightly linked to its security. As businesses become more digitized, they also become more vulnerable to cyber threats. Investing in robust data analytics and cybersecurity measures is non-negotiable for companies aiming to thrive in the digital age.

Another essential measure is fostering partnerships and collaborations. The complexity and scope of digital transformation often require expertise beyond what's available within your organization. Forming strategic partnerships with tech companies, joining industry consortia, and even collaborating with competitors can provide access to new technologies, insights, and markets. These alliances can be critical to navigating future digital shifts successfully.

Customer-centricity should be at the heart of your digital transformation strategy. The digital age has empowered consumers like never before, with expectations for personalized experiences, seamless service, and instant gratification. Businesses that leverage digital technologies to enhance customer engagement and satisfaction are more likely to retain their clientele and attract new customers in the evolving market landscape.

Implementing scalable digital infrastructure is also crucial. As your business embraces more digital solutions, ensuring that your technological infrastructure can support growth and adapt to new advancements is essential. Investing in scalable solutions can prevent bottlenecks and redundancies, facilitating a smoother transition during each wave of digital disruption.

Don't forget the importance of regulatory compliance and ethical considerations. Digital technologies often outpace the regulations designed to govern their use. Staying informed about relevant legal frameworks, ethical standards, and industry best practices not only helps in mitigating risks but also builds trust with your customers and stakeholders.

Moreover, drawing up a digital transformation roadmap can provide clarity and direction. This strategic document should outline your objectives, timelines, required investments, and milestones. It acts as a blueprint, guiding your organization through the stages of digital transformation while allowing flexibility to adapt to unforeseen challenges and opportunities.

Leadership plays a pivotal role in driving digital transformation. Leaders must not only endorse digital initiatives but also lead by example. Demonstrating a willingness to embrace new technologies, challenge the status quo, and learn from failures can inspire a digital mindset across the organization. Effective leadership involves communicating the vision, mobilizing resources, and guiding the organization through the transformation journey.

Preparing the workforce for digital transformation is another critical element. The shift to a digital paradigm necessitates a workforce equipped with the necessary skills and competencies. This might involve reskilling or upskilling employees, promoting a culture of lifelong learning, and recruiting talent with specialized digital expertise. An agile and skilled workforce is a significant asset in the face of digital shifts.

Measuring the impact of digital initiatives is vital for continuous improvement. Establishing key performance indicators (KPIs) for digital transformation efforts can help in assessing their effectiveness, identifying areas for improvement, and demonstrating value to stakeholders. Measurement should be an ongoing process, adapting as objectives evolve and new technologies emerge.

Above all, maintain a customer-centric perspective throughout the digital transformation process. Keeping the customer's needs, preferences, and feedback at the forefront ensures that digital initiatives remain aligned with market demands. This not only enhances customer satisfaction but also drives innovation and growth.

In conclusion, preparing your business for future digital shifts requires a multifaceted strategy encompassing cultural change, technological adoption, strategic partnerships, and continuous improvement. By staying informed, adaptable, and customer-focused, business leaders can navigate the complexities of digital transformation and harness its potential for lasting success. In the dynamic digital landscape, the readiness to evolve is your greatest asset.

Chapter 12:
Seizing the Opportunities
of Digital Transformation

In a world where the only constant is change, digital transformation stands as the emblem of innovation and progress for businesses eager to not just survive but thrive. The journey through the digital frontier, as explored in the preceding chapters, is fraught with challenges yet brimming with opportunities. As we conclude this exploration, it's imperative for business leaders and entrepreneurs to embrace the digital transformation with a strategy that is as fluid as the technology driving the change.

The essence of digital transformation lies in its ability to revolutionize the way businesses operate, deliver value to customers, and position themselves in a competitive marketplace. It's a multifaceted process that encompasses the adoption of digital technology to enhance processes, competencies, and business models. Seizing the opportunities of digital transformation requires a proactive approach, an innovative mindset, and a commitment to perpetual learning and adaptation.

Leading a successful digital transformation involves more than just integrating the latest technologies into your business operations. It demands a deep understanding of your current organizational culture, the readiness to embrace new ways of working, and the foresight to anticipate the impact of digitalization on your industry. Leadership in the digital era is as much about vision as it is about execution. Leaders must inspire, guide, and cultivate an environment where innovation thrives and where the fear of failure is replaced with the excitement of experimentation.

The digital era has democratized information, giving businesses unprecedented access to data insights that can drive strategic decision-making. Leveraging data and analytics enables businesses to understand their customers more deeply, personalize experiences, and anticipate market trends. However, with great power comes great responsibility. The ethical use of data, respecting privacy, and ensuring security must be paramount in a digital leader's agenda.

Technology such as AI, blockchain, and IoT are not just buzzwords but are foundational elements for driving efficiencies, creating new business models, and disrupting industries. Artificial intelligence, for instance, is transforming customer service through chatbots, personalizing shopping experiences online, and optimizing supply chains. Meanwhile, blockchain is redefining trust and transparency in transactions, and IoT is enabling a level of connectivity that permeates every aspect of our lives. Understanding these technologies, their applications, and their potential impact on your business is crucial.

Adopting digital technology also means rethinking how we approach work. The digital workplace is becoming increasingly flexible, collaborative, and employee-centric, enabling a workforce that is more agile, engaged, and productive. Preparing your workforce for digital transformation involves not only equipping them with the necessary digital skills but also fostering a culture that embraces change, encourages innovation, and values continuous learning.

The shift towards digital requires a comprehensive strategy that aligns with your business's core objectives and customer needs. This strategy should be flexible enough to adapt to the rapid pace of digital change yet robust enough to guide your transformation journey. It's about making deliberate choices on where to invest in digital initiatives, how to innovate business models, and ways to enhance customer engagement through digital channels.

Digital marketing and branding have evolved significantly in the digital age, offering businesses new avenues to reach and engage with their target audiences. The power of social media, content marketing, and digital advertising cannot be overstated. These tools not only enhance brand presence but also enable personalized communication and foster community-building around brands.

Navigating the ethical and legal implications of digital transformation is another critical aspect that businesses must consider. In an era where privacy concerns and data breaches are increasingly common, building trust with your customers by ensuring the security of their data and adhering to regulatory requirements is essential. Ethical considerations should be at the heart of your digital initiatives, guiding not only what you can do with technology but what you should do.

Success in the digital era is not just about adopting new technologies but about transforming your organization to become more adaptive, responsive, and innovative. The case studies presented in this book offer valuable lessons from businesses that have successfully navigated their digital transformation journeys. These stories underscore the importance of a clear vision, a strong leadership commitment, and a customer-centric approach in driving digital success.

Looking ahead, the next wave of digital disruption is already on the horizon. Emerging technologies such as 5G, quantum computing, and augmented reality promise to further transform the digital landscape. Preparing your business for these future shifts means staying informed, being flexible, and remaining open to new possibilities. It involves not just keeping up with technological advancements but also anticipating how these changes will shape your industry, your business, and society at large.

The opportunities for businesses willing to embrace digital transformation are boundless. It offers a pathway to innovation, competitiveness, and growth. Yet, seizing these opportunities requires more than just technology adoption; it demands a fundamental shift in how businesses view and approach change. It's about cultivating a mindset that views every challenge as an opportunity for innovation and every failure as a lesson in resilience.

As we close this discussion, it's clear that the journey of digital transformation is ongoing. The landscape of digital technology is ever-evolving, and so too must our strategies for navigating it. For forward-thinking business leaders and entrepreneurs, the message is clear: the time to act is now. Embrace the digital transformation with an open mind and a strategic vision, and you will unlock a world of opportunities. Let your journey through the digital frontier be guided by curiosity, fueled by innovation, and enriched by the endless possibilities that digital transformation offers.

In conclusion, seizing the opportunities of digital transformation is not merely about survival in the digital age—it's about thriving. It's about leveraging the power of digital technology to create value, foster innovation, and drive progress. It's a call to action for businesses to not just anticipate the future but to shape it. As you move forward, remember that the power to transform your business in the digital era lies within. With strategic vision, leadership, and a commitment to innovation, there is no limit to what you can achieve. The future is digital, and it's yours to shape.

Appendix A:
Tools and Resources for Digital Leaders

In the journey through the digital landscape, your compass and map are defined by the knowledge you possess and the tools at your disposal. The aim of this section is to compile a valuable repository of tools and resources to guide digital leaders and entrepreneurs. These offerings are tailored to enhance your strategic vision and operational capabilities, enabling not only the embrace of digital transformation but also the thriving within its tides.

Further Reading and Online Resources

Empowering yourself with the latest insights and forecasts in the digital realm is crucial. Here's a curated list of resources to keep you at the forefront:

Harvard Business Review – Digital Transformation: A collection of articles and insights focusing on the strategies and leadership necessary for digital transformation.

MIT Sloan Management Review – Digital: Provides thought leadership and rigorous research on the management implications of the digital economy.

The Digital Transformation Playbook: This book offers actionable guidance on how to navigate the digital age's unprecedented challenges.

Key Tools for Implementing Digital Strategies

Implementing digital strategies requires not just visionary thinking but practical tools. Here are some key tools that can facilitate this journey:

Google Analytics: Essential for understanding customer behavior on your digital platforms. Insights gleaned can guide your digital marketing strategies.

Slack: Enhances collaboration within teams, breaking down silos and speeding up the flow of information in a digital workplace.

Trello or Asana: These project management tools can help keep your digital transformation projects on track, facilitating task assignment and progress tracking.

HubSpot: A comprehensive platform for digital marketing, sales, and service software, providing a full stack of tools to improve customer engagement and experience.

Tableau: For data visualization, making the complex simple and actionable. Tableau can help you transform your data into strategic insights.

In conclusion, the tools and resources outlined in this section are designed to equip you for a successful digital transformation journey. Embrace these offerings with an open and innovative mindset, and let them serve not just as aids but as catalysts for change and growth. Remember, the landscape of digital technology is ever-evolving, and staying informed and adaptable is key to navigating this dynamic environment successfully.

Further Reading and Online Resources

The landscape of digital transformation is ever-evolving, with new insights, tools, and paradigms emerging at a rapid pace. To stay ahead, it's crucial for business leaders and entrepreneurs to immerse themselves in a continuous learning journey. This section provides a curated list of further reading and online resources that will deepen your understanding of digital transformation and empower you to lead with confidence in this digital era.

Digital transformation isn't just about adopting new technologies; it's about rethinking business models and strategies to leverage these technologies effectively. Books such as "The Digital Transformation Playbook" offer actionable insights into navigating this complex landscape. They provide frameworks that can be tailored to your business context, helping you to redefine value creation in a digital age.

Staying updated with the latest research and thought leadership can give you an edge. Journals like the "Harvard Business Review" and platforms such as "MIT Sloan Management Review" regularly feature articles by leading scholars and practitioners on digital transformation. These resources dissect the latest trends, strategies, and case studies, offering valuable perspectives on implementing successful digital innovations.

Online courses have democratized access to knowledge, with platforms like Coursera and edX offering courses on digital transformation, blockchain, AI, and more. These courses, often developed in collaboration with top universities and industry leaders, provide not just theoretical frameworks but also practical insights and tools. They can be a valuable resource for both you and your team to gain new skills relevant to your digital journey.

Blogs and forums dedicated to tech and innovation, such as TechCrunch and Wired, are also invaluable resources. They not only keep you informed about the latest technological advancements but also provide critical analyses and opinions that can spark new ideas. Following these can help you anticipate trends and make informed decisions about technology adoption.

Social media platforms, particularly LinkedIn and Twitter, have emerged as crucial hubs for digital thought leadership. Following industry leaders and influencers can provide daily bursts of insight and inspiration. Engaging with these communities also offers networking opportunities that can lead to partnerships and collaborations.

Podcasts are an excellent medium for consuming information on the go. Shows dedicated to the intersection of business and technology can offer diverse viewpoints that enrich your understanding. They often feature interviews with innovators and leaders who have successfully navigated digital transformation, providing real-world insights and lessons learned.

White papers and reports from leading technology companies and consulting firms offer in-depth research on digital trends, tools, and best practices. These documents can be gold mines for understanding specific technologies' potential impacts and how other organizations have successfully levered them for growth.

For more interactive learning, webinars and online workshops can provide opportunities to engage with experts and peers. These sessions often cover topical issues and offer Q&A sessions that allow you to dive deeper into subjects that interest you.

Don't overlook the power of networking. Online forums and professional groups bring together like-minded individuals facing similar challenges in digital transformation. Engaging in these communities can provide support, advice, and shared learning that is invaluable.

For those looking to get hands-on with technology, open-source projects and hackathons can be incredibly enlightening. Participating in these can offer practical experience with new technologies and methodologies, further enhancing your understanding and capabilities.

Consider subscribing to newsletters from leading digital transformation consultancies and tech companies. These regularly curated contents can serve as a steady stream of industry insights, trends, and case studies, delivered directly to your inbox.

Lastly, it's vital to remember that digital transformation is as much about people as it is about technology. Resources that focus on change management, leadership in the digital age, and fostering a culture of innovation are just as important as technical guides. Books and articles that delve into these aspects can provide strategies for leading your organization through transformative change effectively.

In conclusion, the journey through digital transformation is ongoing and dynamic. Leveraging the wealth of resources available can help you navigate this journey with greater confidence and success. Remember, the goal isn't just to adopt new technologies but to use these tools to create tangible value for your customers and your business. With the right knowledge and strategies, you can lead your organization into a prosperous digital future.

As we move forward, it's imperative to not only keep abreast of the latest developments but also to critically evaluate how these can be integrated into your business model for sustainable growth. The resources listed in this section are your gateway to evolving as a digital leader, equipped to face the challenges and seize the opportunities that lie ahead in the digital landscape.

Key Tools for Implementing Digital Strategies

In the journey towards digital transformation, the tools and resources at your disposal can significantly dictate the pace and effectiveness of your strategy. In this critical phase, identifying and deploying the right technological tools is not just an advantage; it's a necessity. Let's explore key tools that can help implement your digital strategies, ensuring your organization doesn't just survive but thrives in the digital age.

Digital Project Management Platforms stand at the forefront of essential digital tools. These platforms, like Asana, Trello, and Monday.com, provide a birds-eye view of project timelines, deliverables, and responsibilities. What makes them indispensable is their ability to foster collaboration and streamline workflows, breaking down the silos that often hinder organizational agility.

Next up, we delve into the world of Customer Relationship Management (CRM) systems, such as Salesforce and HubSpot. CRMs collect and organize customer data across various touchpoints. By centralizing information, they empower businesses to tailor experiences to customer preferences and history, driving sales and improving customer satisfaction. In a landscape where customer loyalty is gold, a robust CRM system is your treasure map.

Data Analytics Tools, like Google Analytics and Tableau, also play a pivotal role in digital strategy implementation. These tools provide actionable insights by analyzing patterns in data. From website traffic to patient health records, the application of data analytics spans industries, unlocking opportunities for optimization and innovation.

Collaboration Tools have become the backbone of the digital workplace. Platforms such as Slack, Microsoft Teams, and Zoom not only facilitate communication but also foster a culture of collaboration. In today's remote and hybrid work environments, these tools bridge the physical divide, ensuring teams remain cohesive and productive.

Content Management Systems (CMS), including WordPress and Drupal, are critical for businesses looking to manage their digital content seamlessly. A CMS simplifies the process of creating, managing, and optimizing website content, enabling businesses to maintain an active online presence without extensive technical expertise.

For those navigating the digital marketplace, E-commerce Platforms like Shopify and Magento offer a streamlined, customizable approach to online retail. These platforms provide businesses with the tools to build a comprehensive online store, including inventory management, payment processing, and customer service functionalities.

Cloud Computing Services, such as AWS and Google Cloud, offer scalable resources for data storage, computing power, and networking. By leveraging the cloud, businesses can reduce IT costs, increase flexibility, and accelerate innovation, deploying digital solutions without the need for extensive hardware investments.

Cybersecurity Tools are non-negotiable in the digital age. Solutions from companies like Symantec and McAfee protect data and networks from breaches, ensuring the trust and confidence of customers and stakeholders. As digital strategies become increasingly centered around data, safeguarding this asset is paramount.

Artificial Intelligence (AI) and Machine Learning Platforms are revolutionizing how we solve complex problems and predict future trends. Tools like IBM Watson and Google AI provide businesses with the capabilities to automate tasks, personalize customer experiences, and make data-driven decisions.

Lastly, the importance of Innovation Management Tools cannot be understated. Platforms like Spigit and Brightidea facilitate the generation, evaluation, and implementation of innovative ideas. They provide a structured approach to innovation, ensuring that creative solutions are not just encouraged but effectively executed.

The digital landscape is complex and ever-changing. However, with the right tools in your arsenal, navigating this terrain becomes not just feasible, but exciting. Each of these key tools brings something unique to the table, from enhancing operational efficiency to unlocking new avenues for growth and innovation.

As you move forward in your digital transformation journey, remember that the strength of your strategy doesn't solely lie in the technologies you adopt but in how you apply them to solve real-world problems, meet customer needs, and achieve your business objectives.

It's also crucial to stay agile and receptive to new technologies as they emerge. The digital frontier is expansive and continuously evolving, offering new tools and solutions that can further enhance your digital strategy. Keeping abreast of these developments and being ready to integrate new tools into your ecosystem can provide a competitive edge.

Embracing these tools requires not just technical acumen but a visionary mindset. Leaders must not only understand the potential of each tool but also foster a culture that embraces digital transformation at every level. It's a journey of continuous learning, adaptation, and most importantly, leadership.

In conclusion, the digital era presents a plethora of challenges but, more importantly, unlimited opportunities. The key tools for implementing digital strategies outlined here are your compass and map in this journey. Use them wisely, and you'll navigate the digital frontier not as a traveler but as a trailblazer, unlocking new potentials and leading your organization into a prosperous digital future.

www.ingramcontent.com/pod-product-compliance
Lightning Source LLC
Chambersburg PA
CBHW021146070326
40689CB00044B/1144